A DEEPER SHADE OF
GRACE

A DEEPER SHADE OF GRACE

BERNADETTE KEAGGY

FOREWORD BY PHIL KEAGGY

SPARROW

Sparrow Press
Nashville, Tennessee

Published 1993 in Nashville, Tennessee, by Sparrow Press, and distributed in Canada by Christian Marketing Canada, Ltd.

Printed in the United States of America

97 96 95 94 93   5 4 3 2 1

Library of Congress Cataloging-in-Publication Data

Keaggy, Bernadette.
        A deeper shade of grace / Bernadette Keaggy ; foreword by Phil Keaggy.
           p.   cm.
        ISBN 0-917143-23-X (hard) : $12.95
           1. Consolation. 2. Miscarriage—Religious aspects—Christianity.
    3. Infants (Premature)—Death—Religious aspects—Christianity.
    4. Bereavement—Religious aspects—Christianity. 5. Keaggy,
    Bernadette. 6. Keaggy, Phil. I. Title
    BV4907.K43   1993
    248.8'6—dc20
                                         93-27759
                                         CIP

Quotations and song lyrics in each chapter are from the following:
Ch.1: C.S. Lewis, *The Four Loves*, Harcourt Brace Jovanovich, Inc., 1971.
Ch. 2: "The Answer" by Phil Keaggy © 1971 Archaball Press. All Rights Reserved. Used By Permission.
"Happy Are We" by Phil Keaggy © 1993 Word Music/Sabastina Music. All rights administered by Word Music. All Rights Reserved. Used By Permission.
Ch. 3: "As the Ruin Falls," reprinted from "Poems" by C. S. Lewis. Harcourt, Brace, Javonovich, Inc. © 1964 by The Executors of the Estate of C. S. Lewis.
"Disappointment: His Appointment." Words based on the poem by Edith Lillian Young. Music by Phil Keaggy. © 1976 Birdwing Music (A div. of the Sparrow Corp.) and BMG Songs, Inc. All rights reserved. Used by permission.
Ch. 6: "Carry Your Sorrow No Longer" by Elinor Madeira © 1993 Little Dude Music. All Rights Reserved. Used By Permission.
Ch. 8: "Things I Will Do" by Phil Keaggy © 1976 Birdwing Music (a div. of The Sparrow Corp) and BMG Songs, Inc./Cherry Lane Music Publishing Co, Inc./Sandtree Music. All rights administered by BMG Songs, Inc. All Rights Reserved. Used By Permission. Scripture from Isaiah 42:16 and 43:19.
Ch. 9: "Little Ones" by Phil Keaggy © 1976 Birdwing Music (a div. of The Sparrow Corp) and BMG Songs, Inc./Cherry Lane Music Publishing Co., Inc./Sandtree Music. All rights administered by BMG Songs, Inc. All Rights Reserved. Used By Permission.
"Spend My Life With You" by Phil Keaggy © 1980 Birdwing Musis (a div. of The Sparrow Corp.) and BMG Songs, Inc.,/Cherry Lane Music Publishing Co., Inc./Sandtree Music. All rights administered by BMG Songs, Inc. All Rights Reserved. Used By Permission.
Epilogue: C.S. Lewis, *A Grief Observed*, Faber & Faber, 1966.
"All Our Wishes" by Phil Keaggy © 1993 Word Music/Sabastian Music. All rights administered by Word music. All Rights Reserved. Used By Permission.

All Scripture quotations are from the Holy Bible, New International Version. © 1973, 1978, 1984 International Bible Society. Used by permission of Zondervan Bible Publishers.

Jacket design by Todd Tufts
Book design by Sara Graf Remke

To our five children who did not survive.
We will one day meet again.

FOREWORD

This is a true story, taken from events in our lives. And it's a story that, even though a fair amount of time has passed, is difficult to retell. Why? Because my beloved friend and wife of twenty years has poured her heart and soul into this writing, and I've watched her relive the hopes and dreams, the tragic disappointments and pain of the early years of our marriage, when we wanted children but Bernadette was unable to carry a child to term.

The reason we have opened up this private area of our lives is to bring others *hope*. We have faced tragedy, but we have grown through the pain. We did so because we made a decision earlier in our lives to follow the one who is Love itself—the one who promises that despite the circumstances, he can lead and govern our lives in love.

This Love has a name: Jesus, the Son of God. He is Love itself. When Bernadette and I decided as young adults to give our lives to him, we also committed to obey his simple command: Follow where Love leads—no matter what.

The problem from a human standpoint is that some of the paths he leads us on are frightening and dark.

And sometimes only through tears are we able to see that what we call *darkness* is really a deeper shade of his grace.

Because Bernadette is a gift to me, a warmhearted and compassionate woman, I know that this story—our shared experience, told from her viewpoint—will touch you deeply. This is not a how-to book, with a quick, easy solution to pain. Rather, this book asks you to open your heart at its deepest level and bring the dark and frightening and disappointing out into the light. Bernadette and I know no other way.

But I can also promise you that when you open yourself to Love, he will bring you peace and a stronger sense of grace than you have ever known. He sees the end from the beginning; that is the faith we live in. And so I can say that I'm thankful for all he's led me through as a husband and father, as I look to the author and finisher of my faith.

I encourage you to believe and stake your life on this fact: Our very lives—all of ours—*are* in his hands.

Phil Keaggy
July 1993

ACKNOWLEDGEMENTS

MY THANKS TO:

David Hazard for the time, energy and editing skills he brought to this project, and for continuing to pursue me to write this book.

Kathleen Stephens for her constant encouragement and editorial help.

Elinor Madeira for her willingness to let me share her personal story, and for helping me transcribe many pages of notes.

Debbie Robertson and Maggie Volz for their help in transcribing my notes.

Steve and Amanda Sorenson for their hours of interviewing and for helping put all the events in chronological order.

Phil and our children for their loving support and encouragement and for giving me the time to work on this project. I love you.

When we open
ourselves to love

To love at all is to be vulnerable. Love anything, and your heart will certainly be wrung and possibly be broken. If you want to make sure of keeping it intact you must give your heart to no one, not even to an animal. Wrap it up carefully round with hobbies and little luxuries; avoid all entanglements: lock it up safe in the casket or coffin of your selfishness. But in that casket—safe, dark, motionless, airless—it will change . . . .

—C. S. Lewis, *The Four Loves*

C. S. Lewis, who wrote these words, has a way of pressing his pencil point into my soul. Phil, my husband, loves Lewis's writings, and he was the one who first introduced me to his works. Many know Lewis as the Oxford literature professor who achieved international fame, before his death in 1963, for his outspoken defense of a truly spiritual Christianity. Lewis's public life was much different from ours, of course, but in the personal realms of our lives, similar circumstances often overlap. Most especially, we share the pain that comes when we open our hearts to love and then find ourselves nearly crushed by loss and grief.

In Lewis's case, he fell in love very late in life. In the first months of his marriage, his new wife, Joy, was discovered to be seriously ill with cancer. She died one year later.

Phil and I experienced the loss of our own dreams. We wanted children. We risked our hearts by loving the new lives that grew within me. And when you risk that much—when you risk your own heart—you are most vulnerable to pain. That was why, during the times of greatest pain, Lewis's words came as if they were personal, private notes from a compassionate friend. He wrote with spiritual insight, and also with honesty about the human feelings that nearly overwhelm you when your soul is being broken.

Friends like Lewis are the kind who help you to go back and re-examine your life—the high spots, and the low, dark places too. They help you to understand what you first expected from living, and help you to see why you were so unprepared for the hard punches that get you when you're not looking. They help you to see yourself honestly, right where you are standing, and then they show you how to move up a step to a higher, stronger place.

Phil and I hope we can pass along the same gift of friendship to women and men whose personal struggles are similar to ours. Who doesn't want to always feel the warm, gracious smile of Providence? But we know it's not always like that. Sometimes you need someone who can help you to recognize a deeper shade of grace.

All that Phil and I really wanted was a good marriage based on love and honesty. We didn't want much beyond that, except a few children to share our love with—children with our eyes and characteristics, and our enjoyment of life. I never thought that either a good marriage or a family would be that hard to create.

After all, I was given a pretty great start, as far as a good home life is concerned.

Akron, Ohio, when I grew up there in the 1950s and '60s, still had that small-town, middle-America simplicity. People were mostly innocent and trusting. We never felt we had to lock our doors, because we were just "safe." But mainly, I think, my security came from being raised in a home that was built on a solid marriage between my father and mother, who loved each other a lot.

There were things about our household that made you feel things were always going to be *okay*.

My father, Vic Markwell, was an insurance agent who worked independently and had an office in our home. I grew up seeing my dad at his work, and I admired him for his personal integrity. For one thing, he was a man of his word. He made promises and kept them. He couldn't imagine *not* repaying a debt. He took other people at their word too, risky as that was. I think people always paid Dad their premiums—eventually, even if they got behind—because he trusted them and they wanted to repay that trust.

So, from Dad, I picked up the idea that if you are a good person—if you are faithful, hardworking and do the right thing—then you will seldom be disappointed. You could trust, and that trust would be repaid.

My dad instilled in me another value—the importance of family. Every weekday and many evenings, he worked hard to provide for us, but on weekends he avoided business if at all possible. No calls. No appointments. Then his attention centered on us—that is, on me, and my brother, Don, and my two sisters, Maureen and Mary Rita. Dad loved the outdoors, and many of our weekends were spent together at nearby Virginia Kendall Parks. In the winter, we'd bomb our trusty Radio Flyer sleds down the long slopes, or we'd slip on skates and glide over the frozen rinks. As spring came, Dad took us to launch our new kites, and in summer we'd hike the pine-scented forest. Dad wanted to pass on to us his love of life.

That was how I first felt confident that my life was under the care and protection of a compassionate father.

Mom gave to me a similar, basic trust. She was a nurse who was never off-duty when it came to caring for people.

For instance, there was an endless stream of kids who came to our back door for Band-Aids and a kind word from the woman they called "Bernie." No one left without a bag of treats. Mom also had a following of dear old ladies who stopped by "just to chat." There were cups of tea or coffee offered, and inevitably the conversation led to: "Oh, by the way, Bernie, I've been a little headachy lately. Would you mind checking my blood pressure?"

But Mom's best care she reserved for her children.

There was something soothing and nurturing about the way she took care of us.

Once, for instance, when I was little, I had an especially nasty case of the stomach flu. For days, I was flushed with fever, and no medicine could ease the violent wrenching that grabbed my stomach almost hourly. Mom fed me pieces of chipped ice to fight off dehydration. But best of all, I remember her touch. When I was most miserable, she sat at the edge of my bed, slowly rubbing my back, singing my favorite songs. Her tender touch somehow quieted me, and I fell into a peaceful sleep.

I grew up knowing what it meant to be loved— something that is, unfortunately, rare. Because I felt safe, it was easy for me to trust.

Overall, I've come to believe that a higher influence was at work from my earliest days. It was as if a voice inside said to me, *It's good to know that you're loved and cared for. Trust in someone who loves you, and you won't be disappointed.*

Slowly, I became aware of a harsher side of the world. Looking back, I can see the other influences— ones that taught me to respond to fear and difficult circumstances by building walls inside me for protection.

When we pushed Dad too far, we knew it immediately by the color that flushed into his cheeks and by the jarring slam of his office door where he went to cool off. Rather than risk saying something destructive, I suppose, Dad took his anger and shut it in with him. Mom made herself busy in the kitchen. They never fought in front of us, probably because they believed that parents, not children, should bear stressful loads.

So we learned to tip-toe around the hard matters, while everyone calmed down. Then came the apologies, and the hugs. Balance and order was restored.

But I wasn't sure what to do with the difficult feelings that were left inside me. I felt in the dark about that. And so I shut them away.

We were Catholic, and when I celebrated my first communion my parents gave me a wonderful gift—a beautiful blue 26-inch bike!

When I rode down the brick road in front of our house my heart was pumping with excitement. I felt like I'd arrived. My friends *had* to see me!

Up the street, some neighbors had gathered along the sidewalk to chat. I stopped to adjust a sandal strap. And as I stood there straddling my new bike, a neighbor girl walked over from the group. She began to jump around, and for some reason she *smacked* into the corner of my wire basket. She let out a scream, and I looked up to see a red gush of blood.

The girl's mother was on me before I knew what hit me.

"Why don't you watch where you're going, you clumsy ox," she said to me. "That darn bike is way too big for you."

The girl was still howling, and I dropped my bike and ran all the way home. I wanted to hide my embarrassment and hurt, and I ran all the way to my bedroom.

My sister, Maureen, who was sixteen at the time, gently knocked on the bedroom door. She held me, and tried to reassure me everything would be okay. Later, when I had stopped crying, she talked me into going to retrieve my bike.

Mostly, I was bewildered. How do you comprehend that even if you're cruising along minding your own business, unfair things will happen to you?

Looking back, I can also see how a hard shell begins to form around your tender heart. A shell you could call *selfishness*. Mom tried hard to give me a compassionate outlook toward other people. But something inside me resisted.

On my ninth birthday, for instance, I invited every girl in my class at St. Hedwig's Catholic School to come to our house for a slumber party. Every girl, that is, except one—Mary.

Mary's clothes were worn out and colorless, like they'd been passed down through three or four other children before they reached her skinny shoulders. They usually hadn't been washed. Mary seldom bathed, either. Worst of all, she came to school without socks or underwear! I took my clean, neat appearance for granted. All the girls, including me, giggled at Mary behind her back. And play with her at recess? Never!

When Mom found out that I'd excluded Mary from the slumber party, she had other ideas. "If you don't invite her," she said, "there isn't going to be a party."

We fought over that one. Eventually, grudgingly, I gave in, so I could have the party.

The other girls were surprised to see Mary there. I mostly ignored her. And when Mom gave her a pair of my pajamas and my undies to sleep in, I bit my lip, wanting to say, "No, not my stuff!" Mary's face lit up in a smile, no thanks to me. She wanted friends; she wanted to be loved and to love.

I felt ashamed. But we never did become friends.

Mom believed that every life is sacred. Our faith taught us that. But as I grew up, there were many times I merely side-stepped "unfortunate" people like Mary. Why did I hold back, when a simple act of kindness and friendship could have helped someone through a lonely struggle? What was I trying to protect, there inside my shell?

On the other side of the coin, when you build a protective shell around yourself, you may also keep out something that would be good for you.

Only later would I learn what it's like to feel like an outsider.

When you become a teenager, it's amazing how hard that shell of *self* can get. My expectations were highest and my tolerance lowest when it came to religion.

The Catholic-school environment taught me to respect the priests and nuns, because they had given their lives to serve God. Priests were next to God, and the nuns were supposed to be like saints. How could anyone live up to that kind of expectation for long?

As a teenager, I had a hyper-awareness of every flaw in people. When the priests got angry and yelled, or when the nuns made a mistake or cried, there was no room in my thinking for them to be human. I thought truly spiritual people were above feeling pain. Their faith carried them over trials, and they never needed love or understanding. They were icons.

In a way, it was natural to think this. Our faith emphasized the awesomeness and magnitude of God. This gave me a high respect for him. But I didn't see how God could be a part of my everyday life. My own human failings were so glaring. All our teaching emphasized sin, and all that separated me from God. How could I be a Christian when I was constantly faced with all the wrong things in my life?

I guess I equated God with rules and regulations: Don't eat meat on Friday. Wear your dresses long enough. Don't question people in authority; they're always right.

Who wants to think about God, when it only makes you feel bad about yourself?

I walked into junior high school feeling a bit critical and case-hardened about religion. And it was easy to toss religion aside, because the youth culture of the late-'60s was exploding. Everyone was searching for reality—for people to be the same on the inside as they were on the outside.

Almost overnight, I rejected the "Catholic girl" image. As I walked straight into "hippiedom," my moral values went out the window.

My parents must have ached to see our simple, innocent way of life swept away overnight. In the space of a few months, my brother Don was shipped off to Vietnam, Maureen left home "to find herself," and Mary Rita faced marriage and pregnancy at nineteen.

And as for me . . . I put a lot of energy into pushing my parents away. *Me first*—that was my motto.

Yes, you can surround yourself with walls, even working to keep out those who love you the most. And you never think about the person you're becoming as you close yourself in . . . or how dark it's really getting in your small, self-centered world.

$\int$ometimes a new kind of light surprises you, coming at the most unexpected time or place.

Every weekend, my friend Sharon and I sneaked off to a couple of local bars. One was called Oden's Den, and the other was J. B.'s Club. Because Sharon was three years older, and because she was a friend of the family, my parents trusted us together. They would have died if they'd known I was using my sister's I.D. to get into the clubs, because I was still several years underage. Not that we drank alcohol—we went to hear the bands.

Oden's Den was a perfect name for this place. It was dark and loud and smoky, and swarming with people. The first time we went there we heard a band that was becoming really popular—a group called Glass Harp. They'd toured throughout Ohio and Pennsylvania, and were opening for some of the top recording bands of the day. Sharon and I managed to find one tiny square of floor space to squeeze into.

When Glass Harp came on, they began to crank out some of the hottest rock and roll I'd ever heard! Their music was incredible, and the lyrics had something to say.

But mostly, I was attracted to the lead guitarist, who was also the lead singer. Phil Keaggy was slightly built, with a dark beard and mustache . . . and large, kind eyes. I immediately felt attracted to him, not only because of his looks and talent, but for other reasons. Even up there on the stage, there was something different about him—a charisma, and a brightness of spirit. He didn't give off that arrogant, *come-and-get-me-girls* air of a rocker.

When Glass Harp finished the set, Phil came down from the stage. Yes, I wanted to meet him. No, I did not want to introduce myself. No doubt, one of those girls hanging around the front of the stage had to be his girlfriend.

But as Phil maneuvered through the crowd, he had to dodge a guy standing next to us, and he turned right into me. As if I was meant to be in *that* place at *that* time, I was eye-to-eye with him. Our eyes connected, and something deeper too.

"Hi, I'm Phil Keaggy," he said, almost surprised. "Um . . . would you like a cough drop?"

That was how this talented but unassuming man was ushered into my life.

Later that evening, after the show, I was amazed when he invited me to a friend's house. There I met some of the nicest people I'd ever run into.

No one was doing drugs. There were no couples tucked off in dark corners, hanging all over each other. Everyone was sitting in a circle, singing songs and reading from the Bible. And they were having a grand time.

I was in awe. There was something different here. The whole vibe of these people was happy, friendly, open. By contrast, I felt so cautious and closed. When you're trying hard to be "cool" you never let your guard down.

Phil Keaggy was a breath of fresh air, and from the beginning I think I knew he was going to open up the self-centered shell my heart was locked in.

Besides Phil's easy manner and great sense of humor, there was a certain way he talked about his spiritual beliefs—so naturally, without religious talk. He seemed to possess something that no one else had ever offered me. It was a sense of hope and promise.

"When you open your heart to God," Phil would say, "you find out he's the only one who will never let you down."

Trust God? Open your heart to him? That was a totally new concept to me. From the start, Phil and I talked a lot about his faith. He made it sound real and exciting, not like religious drudgery. I thought of myself as an open person, too, and Phil made me want to believe.

It was like a whole new realm opening up to me. Phil believed in something that challenged me to reach out beyond myself, and I felt ready for the risk.

In the weeks after I met him, I felt drawn to this new kind of Christian faith and wanted to trust God with my whole life, the way Phil did.

How could I guess what would come from this "chance" meeting of Phil Keaggy? I was open to the idea that a new page of my life was about to be written—and totally unaware that the full story was beyond my power to create. After all, I knew what I wanted from life, and thought I knew how to get it.

I was unaware, though, that there was another, higher plan for my life—a kind of story I could never conceive.

"We'll be forever singing..."

Mom and Dad were in shock.

Phil and I had quickly grown in our friendship, and his influence was so strongly positive that I couldn't stop telling my family about him. He was so decent and so different from the shady characters I'd been going out with—and *that* was a welcome relief for my parents. But mostly, they were amazed that I had done such a dramatic turnaround. For more than a year, my relationship with them had been strained, and now I was letting them back into my private world again.

You can imagine how curious they were about this guy who had such a dramatic effect on me. They were eager to meet him.

The first time Phil swung into our driveway in his little sports car—with a guitar in the passenger seat—I knew I had Mom and Dad's attention. That certain *set* of Dad's jaw told me what he was thinking: *Who is this older guy—a musician no less, with a sports car—and what does he want with my fifteen-year-old daughter?*

In no time at all, Phil sat himself down on the sofa to chat with Dad. I could tell by the way Dad nodded and chuckled at Phil's good humor that a few walls were down. And when Phil talked openly about the car accident only a year earlier in which his mother had been killed, Dad became all fatherly and kind. I watched his interest sharpen when Phil told how that tragedy changed his life.

At the funeral, Phil's older sister, Ellen, told him the meaning of the Christian gospel and how you could come into relationship with God. Ellen told him that God loved us so much that he sent his only son, Jesus, to die on the cross for us. Because he laid down the lifeblood of his only son, God himself made a way for us to come back to him.

"When Ellen explained the Christian message to me that way," Phil said, "it was easy to see how I had misunderstood God. Misunderstood what being a Christian was all about. I thought it was just rules, rules and more rules. I thought that God was waiting to nail me every time I did something wrong."

Dad listened intently.

"But my sister helped me see that God is much different than what I'd thought," he went on. "God has laws—but he's given those laws so that we can live the right way and be protected from things that can harm us. And he loves us. He wants us to trust him, and live close to him. His heart is open toward us, and Jesus's death on the cross is proof of that."

Phil told Dad that Ellen had encouraged him to put his life in God's hands, and to experience the peace that he'd find from trusting God the way you would trust a loving father. "When I made the decision to do that," Phil said, "everything changed—including my music."

I could tell that all of this was a relief for Dad and Mom, because they knew Phil was a "rocker." And, to be honest, I was listening to what Phil was saying too—first, because I wanted to know if there was something bigger and better than the little world I felt caged in, and second, because of the gentle non-preachy way he talked about it.

He made it sound simple and real. And he didn't seem to think that he was better than me because of what he believed.

When Phil was not on road trips with Glass Harp, we squeezed in every hour together that we could find. He would drive up from his flat in Youngstown, an hour away, and we'd take long walks in the hills nearby.

Mostly, I asked questions and listened. I knew that the peace and goodness Phil talked about was exactly what I wanted.

Oddly, I still felt some resistance to all this in my heart, even though it sounded good. When I was aware of it at all, I couldn't explain my urge to hold back—not even to myself.

Phil introduced me to the Bible during this time. He showed me, through the Bible, how all God's anger at our sin and failure was taken care of by Jesus's death on the cross. Our part was to respond to God's offer of a new life, so that we could enjoy his love. One passage of Scripture that struck me was written by a man who was probably Jesus's closest friend and follower. In a letter, John wrote:

> This is how God showed his love among us: He sent his one and only Son into the world that we might live through him. This is love: not that we loved God, but that he loved us, and sent his son as an atoning sacrifice for our sins . . . We love because he first loved us. (1 John 4:9–10, 19)

I felt I was not hearing of "religion" as I'd known it, but of a new way that lay open to me. Phil said that when I trusted God, and committed my life to him, God would begin to make himself real to me.

All of this spoke to me right where I was, and something inside urged me to take a risk, to take the crucial first step.

Slowly, over the period of a few months in 1971, I decided to take that step.

Everything changes, although not always as you expect.

Some of my old friends began to feel uncomfortable around me—not that I waved a Bible at them, but mostly because I was changing and not really interested in the old lifestyle anymore.

Something else changed too. There was a new atmosphere between my parents and me. And it felt good and right.

Phil was a perfect gentleman to me and to my parents. He always took time to visit with Mom and Dad when he drove out to see me, and he learned that Dad was a big music fan, and had once played drums in a big band. Dad's wariness about this young musician turned to delight at having a kindred spirit around.

Somehow, throughout the winter and spring of 1972, Phil kept closing the gap between me and my parents. Partly because he was older, I think, and partly because of his mother's death, Phil knew the importance of family. That touched a deep chord in me.

I wanted to know more and more about this guy who was a rock-and-roll guitarist and songwriter *and* a Christian.

As for Phil's career, Glass Harp recorded its third album for Decca Records in New York City in late spring, 1972. Now that they had fulfilled their contract, Phil decided to tell the other guys he would be leaving the band soon. Several things influenced his decision. For one thing, he had been on his own most of the time since he was sixteen. He'd lived a multitude of places without his family, for the sake of working in bands and doing what he loved most. But his taste for wandering was changing, partly because our friendship and fondness for each other was growing deeper the more time we spent together. Phil's leaving the band was agonizing for everyone involved, because Glass Harp had had big plans for touring in new areas of the country.

But more than anything, Phil felt that he could no longer live the crazy, rock-and-roll life *and* live out his Christianity at the same time. Through songs like "The Answer," he had been able to share his faith on the group's albums and even at some of the wildest rock concerts. In part, the words went like this:

. . . with this feeling of love in my heart,
my Lord is with me always.
And though I know this is just a start,
there are no more dark hallways.
In praise and cheer we're gathered here
with many or with few.
I saw the light, and now tonight
you can see it too.

The answer—you don't need to be alone anymore.
The answer—is Jesus, believe me, he'll open the door . . .

Still, Phil wanted the freedom to play more of his own Christian music, and he wanted to play to new audiences.

Then there was *us*. Our deepening relationship was beginning to conflict with Phil's grueling schedule. Some decisions had to be made.

"Bernadette," Phil once said to me, "you are my quiet place."

That was when I think I knew . . .

Phil's popularity was growing, and we were both being caught up in the wave of young people who in the early '70s turned from hippiedom to faith in God. Now Phil was being asked to play acoustical guitar sets at youth rallies, churches and colleges. He was welcomed to sing and speak freely of his faith.

In the fall of my senior year of high school, Phil finally asked my parents for my hand in marriage. A number of my friends were leery of my getting married so young. I knew that by my marrying at eighteen the odds were against us. Yet I honestly felt this was God's design, and that I was making the right choice. By now

I had adopted this simple, open kind of faith that Phil Keaggy brought into my life. I would trust God for our marriage, for my life.

On July 14, 1973, having just returned my graduation robe, I put on a white satin gown that I had sewn myself. Mom set the ring of red roses on my head, and I walked happily down the aisle, my arm in Dad's. As we moved together, Phil began to sing a song he wrote for me.

> *Your smile makes me warm inside.*
> *Your hand in my hand, we'll walk,*
> *and in Him we'll abide.*
> *Happy are we.*
> *Happy are we.*
>
> *And we'll be forever*
> *singing—He's bringing our hearts,*
> *closer together.*
> *Bernadette, I love you,*
> *you love me.*
> *A little corner on a hill is where*
> *we said our prayer.*
> *The day is gone, the night is still,*
> *and we could feel Him there.*

Our love is a deep fountain
of caring and sharing,
a new life from above
Happy are we.
Happy are we.

There at the altar, we knew our lives were going to be as perfect as our wedding day. We began to travel throughout northern California in the fall of 1973. Phil had been asked to play guitar for a popular group called Love Song. He considered this an honor, since they were one of only a few Christian bands making a positive statement with their music.

Family was on our minds a lot. The band traveled together from city to city in a large motor home, and we became one big family with the Coomes, the Truaxes, the Girards and the Mehlers and all their lovely babies and toddlers. Phil and I soaked in their friendship and took mental notes on how these couples raised their children with love and discernment. Maybe it would not be long before there would be little Keaggy children in the world too.

When the tour ended, we halfheartedly returned to Ohio. Here, we would begin our own life of faith together. For eight months, Phil traveled with a young friend and talented guitarist, Peter York, playing wherever they were asked to sing.

Phil decided not to set a fee for concerts, but instead to request only enough to cover their expenses. I was amazed at how each time a bill came that we couldn't pay, a check arrived in the mail sent by someone who had been encouraged by Phil's music and wanted to help support us.

So I began to learn about daily, minute-by-minute faith.

We were determined to live in a way that was wide open to whatever God had for us. We knew he loved us, and we had vowed to show our love for him.

The true test was yet to come.

This is not how it's supposed to be

It was July 1974, and we had been married just a year when we packed up our belongings in a large U-Haul. During our honeymoon, we visited a Christian community called Love Inn, in the rolling farmland of south-central New York State. Now we felt drawn to embark on a new adventure and become a part of that community. The little township of Freeville, where Love Inn was located, sat on the outskirts of the college town of Ithaca. Students came here to attend Cornell University as well as Ithaca College. Here, New York's famed Finger Lakes wrapped around the base of steep hills, and streams gushed from mountain springs.

Scott Ross was the pastor of this fellowship. We had come to know about Love Inn through his syndicated radio broadcast, which dealt with cutting-edge issues of contemporary Christianity. Scott played popular music and integrated into his program the new music being created by Christian musicians such as Love Song, Honeytree and 2nd Chapter of Acts. Phil's first solo album, "What a Day," was becoming a hit with Scott's listeners too. It was exciting to be part of a new wave of young Christian believers who wanted to spread the gospel. And music was the connecting link, because it crossed the borders of resistance and got into people's hearts. Someone who would never attend a church to hear a preacher would easily put on a record and not only enjoy the music but pay attention to its lyrics. When Scott played contemporary songs, he talked about them from a spiritual standpoint, describing how they pointed out the hunger and thirst for reality and true spirituality so many young people felt. In his commentary, Scott always directed them to Jesus Christ.

We were open to whatever God wanted for us, and we felt Love Inn was the place where we could walk out our faith.

The move took us several hundred miles east of home. It felt strange to be away from Mom and Dad, but also exciting! Love Inn was housed in a huge old renovated barn that sat on acres of farmland. The old farmhouse directly next to the barn was owned by a wonderful middle-aged woman named Peg Hardesty, who was part of the fellowship as well. Inside, the barn-turned-studio-and-sanctuary was a collage of col-ored carpet squares, hewn wood and new stained-glass windows. It definitely was not your typical church. Nor were these people typical churchgoers. Young peo-ple of all varieties found their way to Love Inn, all of us wanting to live out our faith in community. We ate together, prayed together, sang together and often worked together. The common thread was that we all believed God was alive and active and still answering prayer.

Phil and I found a small one-story brick house about two miles from the Love Inn property. It had been split into two apartments, and we rented one. Stan and Lonnie Harrington, who also were a part of the fellowship, occupied the other side. I loved unpacking our wedding gifts and putting a home together—even when that meant creatively covering boxes to make end tables or searching out second-hand stores for the perfect ten-dollar couch.

As we settled in, I found myself thriving on our simple, live-by-faith lifestyle. I remember telling Phil he had to raise my grocery budget to $30 a week, because we almost always had extra people for dinner. I didn't have a full-time job because Phil wanted me to travel with him whenever possible. When he was out of town doing concerts and finances were tight, I helped out teaching art classes at the small community school Love Inn had started. We never quite knew how the monthly bills would be paid, let alone the unexpected ones. Phil received small honorariums for his concerts, but the food on our table came mostly from Christians around the country who heard of Love Inn and wanted to be a part of our lives.

I remember thinking, *Someday we'll be on the giving end, and help to support people and organizations that we believe in.*

After about six months, the leaders of the community strongly urged Phil to stop traveling and doing concerts. They felt it was important that he and I build a stronger, more stable relationship and get a better idea of what it meant to be a husband and wife, responsible for the needs of a home and family. Phil did not fully agree that he had to stop traveling altogether to accomplish this, but decided to try it for a time. It was true that the life of a musician and recording artist was anything but normal or consistent.

So Phil helped duplicate tapes for the Scott Ross Show that were sent out weekly to hundreds of radio stations. The work was laborious, but the benefits came when thousands of letters would flood the mail room, each telling a unique story of how God used the show to help someone. We all took turns answering these let-

ters individually. In doing so, we were encouraged ourselves, because God seemed to be doing miracles. Kids
were getting off drugs, and marriages were being sal-
vaged. Then there were the minor miracles in our lives. . . .

During our first winter in Freeville, the cold and
snow were beyond belief. One day I was driving on a
country road in my trusty Volkswagen squareback, trying to avoid large gutters of ice. Through the blowing
snow, I barely could see the road when all of a sudden,
the car spun around, out of control. I ended up side-
ways in a deep ditch. Before I could even take stock of
what happened, two huge men stopped their cars and
got out. To my amazement they literally lifted my car
back onto the road, pulled out my crumpled fender
with their hands, smiled and were gone. I drove in a
state of shock to the barn where Phil was working,
looking like I'd seen a ghost—or an angel. God seemed
to be totally in control of my life, even in unforeseen
circumstances.

Later, we read Psalm 91:11–12: "For he will command his angels concerning you to guard you in all
your ways; they will lift you up in their hands, so that
you will not strike your foot against a stone." It seemed
to us that nothing could touch or harm us inside God's
protection.

We were growing as a couple. Phil and I enjoyed
reading together, whether it was E. Stanley Jones, C. S.
Lewis, Ann Kiemel or the Bible. We also enjoyed having friends over for a meal, then discussing our faith.
Though few of them had children yet, we talked often
about what it would be like. We had great laughs
together as we shared both silly and sobering family
stories.

Phil and I became each other's confidant and support. When he was feeling pressured at work or feeling creatively stunted, we'd talk it through for hours. Then we'd hold hands and pray. Not that things would change immediately, but it helped to voice our thoughts and ideas and to develop patience as well. And I loved the warmth and spiritual closeness of being with this man whom I cherished.

About the time Phil was eager to do a new record and start playing concerts again, we got a call from Buck Herring, producer of the group 2nd Chapter of Acts. He wanted Phil to play guitar on their new album, "In the Volume of the Book." Buck also wanted to produce a record with Phil. Since creatively and musically, Phil was about to burst at the seams, they agreed to work together on Phil's second album. Phil began writing songs, and he formed the Phil Keaggy Band—or PKB—with four other musicians from our area and started touring again. Sometimes the wives traveled with the band, but most often we stayed home, to keep expenses down. I was happy to see him working again at what he knew and loved best, his music.

One song that Phil wrote was based on a poem by C. S. Lewis, who had become our favorite writer. It was called, "As the Ruin Falls," and the words were intriguing to me:

All this is flashy rhetoric about loving you,
I never had a selfless thought since I was born.
I am mercenary and self-seeking through and through;
I want God, you, all friends, merely to serve my turn....

Lewis seemed to be writing about spiritual discovery. Somehow, he understood that even as a Christian, there was still a force inside him that worked contrary to his faith. A Christian is one who willingly submits to God's plan for his or her life. But slowly, subtly, the temptation comes to seek only what we want, and to question God's goodness and wisdom. We can begin to reconstruct walls around our lives—even very spiritual-looking walls made up of all the right external behaviors, like prayer, attending church and Bible reading. And yet inwardly we can remain just as much in control of our lives as ever, and be blind to the fact that we are no longer living as Christians, open to God, trusting God from the heart.

When Phil first sang this song for me, we discussed what Lewis must have meant. We gave God permission to do whatever it took to break down inner walls we might secretly have constructed, walls that would make our hearts hard toward him—even if it caused us great pain. Like Lewis, we wanted to be able to say, *"For this I bless you as the ruin falls—the pains you give me are more precious than all other gains."*

We had been married almost two years, when early one spring morning in 1975, I woke up feeling queasy. The nausea recurred each morning without fail. By the second week, I decided to confirm my suspicions and visit the local women's clinic in Ithaca for a pregnancy test. I saw the doctor, had a blood test and waited for what seemed like forever for the verdict: *positive.*

As I drove home, I was hardly able to contain myself. I burst into our house and into Phil's arms. "We're going to have a baby!" I said.

Immediately, we called my parents, who were thrilled. Then we let our friends in on our great news.

We were in good company, because many of our friends were starting families as well.

This was a tremendous new responsibility for us. Me, a mother? Phil, a father? Was it possible? It happens every day to people—but now it was happening to *us*, and it felt pretty wonderful.

Our neighbor, Lonnie, had just found out she was pregnant as well. As the weeks went by we enjoyed sharing our new experiences with each other. We'd get together for our weekly bread-baking and talk about baby names, who our children would most resemble and compare our expanding bellies.

I went regularly for my monthly checkups and according to the doctors, everything looked fine. Phil often went with me, because he wanted to be a part of every aspect of this child's life. As we listened to the baby's heartbeat grow stronger, we were delighted. A new life was in waiting. There was something sacred about the fact that a child was growing within me. We were in awe about the whole birth process as we read page by page a book on the first nine months of life. It gave us a new awareness of God's magnificent handiwork. Now there was new meaning in Psalm 139:13, which says, "For you created my inmost being; you knit me together in my mother's womb." God was forming this child within me, and I was deeply at peace.

There was something exceptional about the beautiful fall season that settled over New York that year. The trees across the hills were a collaboration of orange, red and yellow. One Saturday, the air was brisk as Phil and I walked hand-in-hand down the tree-lined streets of Freeville. On the way home, we stopped and looked over the huge baskets of apples at a roadside stand and decided on some fresh cider. A flutter inside stopped me. "Phil, quick, put your hand on my side," I said in an excited whisper. "The baby—I felt him kick!"

Phil's eyes were wide as he rested his hands on my stomach.

It was like a first "hello" from this little person who was coming to us from God.

As the weeks passed the flutters gave way to gentle kicks. While I lay still in bed at night, Phil wrapped his arms around me and sang silly little songs.

"Baby, baby you're so sweet. Baby, baby, I feel your feet! Baby, baby, you're so neat!"

This child was going to be musical, I thought, and have a great sense of humor.

As I entered my fifth month of pregnancy, my belly expanded greatly. I talked regularly to my mom on the phone.

"Now Bernadette," she said, "you've got to lie down and take little rests during the day." This was my nurse-mother speaking.

"Yes, Mom, I'll try," I assured her.

She sent me maternity stretch panels to sew into my regular jeans, which were long past fitting. I'd listen to her many stories about when she was pregnant with me, and how her back hurt so. I was glad to be young and healthy and feeling great with this child. We entered a whole new phase of our lives together as mother and daughter. My mom had always had time for a hug, or to listen to the many stories we brought home from school. And I felt God daily stretching my heart too, making room for this little one.

I felt ready for the adventure ahead.

Sunday, November 1, was cold and brisk. Several inches of snow had fallen, not unusual for upstate New York. Bundled up, we headed for the 10 a.m. worship service at the barn. I settled myself into one of the few theater seats that were lined up against the wall. Everyone else sat cross-legged on the carpeted floor. The sun streamed in through the stained-glass windows and left lovely colored patterns throughout the roomful of praying, singing, clapping people. Phil sat on stage, and helped lead the singing.

Ted Sandquist, who was one of the teachers, had

written a lot of worship songs that we all knew by heart:

> *O come, let us worship and bow down!*
> *Let us kneel before the Lord our Maker....*

As I sang along, my mind began to wander. My tummy felt very tight. I started to feel my uterus tightening up. Again. And again. Slowly and consistently. Now I was preoccupied. What was this?

Halfway through the service, I got up and walked to the back of the room to stand against the wall. I tried to put out of my mind any worried thoughts. *It's nothing. I probably didn't sleep as well as I could have last night.* I couldn't wait for the service to end, because I began feeling worse. I made my way to Phil and whispered that I wasn't well and could we head home quickly.

My sudden pains made Phil anxious too, and we called the doctor the minute we got home.

When the nurse finally tracked him down, Dr. Nelson called me back. "So what's the problem?"

"I seem to be having some contractions that are getting uncomfortable," I said.

Casually, he responded, "You're probably experiencing some Braxton-Hicks contractions. That's normal for your fifth month. Try some gentle rocking on your hands and knees. That should cause them to ease up. Call me in the office on Monday if they're still bothering you."

I hung up the phone, and tried to do the exercises he suggested.

The pains worsened.

"Phil, call Lonnie to come over, please," I asked. "I've got to lie down."

When Lonnie walked into the bedroom, there was a concerned look on her face. "What's the matter?" she asked.

By now I was rocking back and forth in agony, unable to answer. All at once I felt like someone let the plug out on me. My water broke and amniotic fluid gushed onto the bedroom floor.

Phil hurriedly dialed the doctor back, as Lonnie held my hand and Stan mopped the floor. The doctor told Phil to head straight for the hospital where he would meet us.

Phil, Lonnie and I hustled into the car and headed for Tompkins County Hospital in Ithaca, about twenty-five minutes away. I winced over every bump Phil tried cautiously to avoid. I had no words for what I was feeling, but my heart was sick with fear.

Oh, little baby, are you all right?

Phil held my hand tightly and prayed out loud, "God, please let everything be all right."

By the time we got to the hospital, my labor was in full swing. The nurses helped me out of the wheelchair and onto the gurney. They quickly got me into a hospital gown and checked me. I was fully dilated. The doctor nodded to the nurse to scrub up as they ushered me into the delivery room. I was thrashing in agony. Fear and panic came over me as they wheeled me into the cold, sterile delivery room. The large swinging doors slammed in Phil's face, leaving him on the outside in total dismay.

This is not how it's supposed to be! I thought. I was overwhelmed by everything. I hadn't even taken a childbirth class yet—that was supposed to start next month.

The nurse was squeezing my arm now, trying to

give me instructions. I was too out of it to really understand her. "Mrs. Keaggy, all I can give you is a local anesthetic," she said. "The baby is so small and is coming quickly."

"Bear down—and push!" another nurse chimed in.

With that, I saw my firstborn son emerge—perfectly silent, unmoving. The doctor laid him on my stomach.

There was utter serenity on his small face....

Suddenly more contractions came, and a second son emerged, still in his amniotic sac. I was in disbelief, and the doctor as well, when several more screaming contractions gave way to yet a third son.

Unlike the others, this little one had an ounce of life in him.

The doctor reached for a large oxygen mask and virtually covered the baby's face, as he held this tiny body in the palm of one hand. In a few minutes, the baby stopped breathing altogether.

It was over. This fast and furious ordeal was over. I looked down at my three small sons, still on my stomach. I studied their perfectly formed bodies. With one hand, I stroked their dark, soft hair. Every detail of their bodies was complete, right down to their eyelashes and and fingernails. Their beautiful bowed lips seemed relaxed and at peace. This was my one and only moment of contact with my sons. I was amazed that all this had gone on inside of me, and my heart was breaking. Tears ran off my chin.

In another moment, I was startled by the nurse removing the babies from me. She said, "The cut-off point for when you have to have a proper burial and funeral is six months. The doctor thinks these babies were about twenty-two weeks. Do you want us to take care of things?"

"Okay," I said.

Physically and emotionally, I was exhausted. Part of me was still in a fog, lost in thought, trying to make sense out of what happened. It didn't register exactly what they would do with the triplets, but the last time I saw my sons, the nurse wheeled them out of the room on a gurney.

When I was taken into recovery, the clock said 6:15 p.m. All this had taken place in a few short hours. Phil was waiting for me, along with our pastor, Ted Sandquist. The doctor had already told Phil the news. I would be okay, but none of our three sons had lived.

Phil cried and hugged me. Ted put his arms around us and quietly prayed. He asked God to give us peace—to help us know that these sons were in his arms and that we would again have children. His words were gentle and strong.

After Ted left, Phil and I held each other. His hand traced over my now-empty abdomen. We both wept as our lives turned upside down. I just wanted to sleep for hours and hours.

The next morning I woke to find Phil softly walking in to my hospital room with a bouquet of flowers. He looked so tired.

"How are you feeling?" he asked.

"Tired, confused, sad," I replied. Phil and I tried to put the puzzle pieces back in place.

"I can't believe it's over. I feel like a displaced father, one day I'm telling friends I'm going to be a papa, the next day I'm not," he said. He'd never even had the chance to see his sons.

"You know, my grandmother German had two sets of twins that died—did I ever tell you that?" I asked.

"No," Phil answered. "Do you think that if you'd been carrying just one child, it would have lived?"

We had so many questions, and no answers.

As I recovered from the shock of what happened, I had to deal with the emotional impact of not burying our sons. Phil didn't carry this burden as much because he never saw the babies and didn't realize what fully-developed human beings they were. But I knew they should have had a proper burial.

What the nurses undoubtedly did with them haunted me—they'd been discarded, just like aborted babies. *If people only knew,* I thought. *If they could have seen them....*

We mustered our courage, and went home. In the days that followed, as I recuperated, a number of friends came to see me. Others tentatively approached me at church or in town. Our friends tried hard to offer encouragement. Losing children was not only a new experience for us, but also for those around us. Some avoided the subject altogether, afraid they'd upset me. In retrospect, I probably acted as though I was doing better than I really was.

One woman, in an attempt to encourage me, said brightly, "Oh don't be upset. You'll get pregnant again."

I began to get a clear picture: people really didn't understand. These children that had died were my own flesh and blood. Even if we did have more children, they would never replace my three firstborn sons.

Another friend said, "Your babies are in heaven. That's something to smile about."

Smile? Is that all that mattered—whether or not I could smile?

For the most part, I kept my thoughts to myself, did my best to pull myself together and went on. But deep down I felt guilty about my grief. I felt like a second-rate Christian, because my arms ached to hold my babies. What was the matter with me?

Lonnie was one of the few who gave me what I needed. Fortunately, she came to see me soon after I got home from the hospital. "Hi, how are you feeling?" she asked cautiously.

"Okay, I guess," I said, concealing the truth.

She handed me a small milk-green vase, with peach silk flowers in it. "I'm sorry," she said.

Then she stood next to my bed, watching my tears flow, not knowing what to say. I knew she was hurting for me—I could see it in her eyes.

Then she said the most amazing thing: "It could have just as easily been me. I know that I don't understand it all either."

I think it was as hard for Lonnie to be around me as it was for me to see her still pregnant. From then on she kept her thoughts of her pregnancy to herself, and was sensitive to my feelings. I appreciated that. Lonnie had a compassion that reached out in total empathy. She wasn't afraid to approach me, even though I could see that it made her uncomfortable. She really wanted to understand the pain I was feeling, and I felt I could cry around her. I had many thoughts and feelings to work through. I kept that little vase of roses, because it symbolized a deep understanding of our loss.

While I dealt with my own feelings, Phil was at a loss for words to express his mixture of pain and loss and faith. Reading through an old book, he found a poem by Edith Lillian Young, called "Disappointment." Phil put the words to music:

Disappointment—HIS appointment, change one letter,
Then I see, that the thwarting of my purpose
  is God's better choice for me.
His appointment must be blessing,
  though it may come in disguise,
For the end from the beginning, open to His wisdom lies.

Disappointment—HIS appointment, whose?
The Lord's who loves me best,
Understands and knows me fully,
  Who my faith and love would test.
For like a loving, earthly parent,
He rejoices when He knows,
That His child accepts unquestioned
  all that from His wisdom flows.

Disappointment—HIS appointment,
Lord I take it then as such,
Like the clay in hands of pottery

yielding wholly to Thy touch.
All my life's plan is Thy molding,
  not one single choice is mine,
Let me answer unrepining
Father not my will but Thine.

...treasures of your love untold. Was this love—to lose three infant sons? I listened, and I agreed. I agreed, that is, because inside, I wanted to believe.

But what was I to do with these other powerful feelings?

Confident about the future

Winter stayed a long time that year. Or so it seemed to me. Spring proved to be very busy though. Phil's first solo album was purchased for release on the newly-formed record label, Newsong, which was distributed by Word Records. He was scheduled to do a three-week acoustic tour with Nancy Honeytree, a female troubadour gifted with gentle words and sweet melodies.

Together they set off with a small road crew and traveled to colleges and churches throughout the midwest. I decided to join them for the second half of the tour, hoping to get my mind off what had happened. Despite the emotional pain that sometimes reared its head, Phil and I felt confident about the future. We relied on each other and believed we could get through this together.

Babies were a sensitive topic for us, one we weren't too comfortable opening our hearts about. Oddly enough, few people—for whatever reasons—ever brought up our loss. This was unfortunate, because it kept us from realizing that we weren't the only ones going through this kind of trauma. Far from it. Later on, we learned that each year around 250,000 couples in the United States alone experience a neonatal death of a child. And amazing as it seems, approximately one in three children conceived each year do not reach their first birthday.

These deaths, I have learned, fall into one of the four major categories that comprise prenatal (fetal/infant death):

•those occuring within the first year of life from an undetermined cause—sudden infant death syndrome (SIDS);

•those occuring during the first six months of life from some known cause—neonatal death;

•stillbirth;

•those occuring during the prenatal period through miscarriage and premature birth.

Some 12,000 to 15,000 babies fall victim to SIDS, and two out of every 100 pregnancies result in stillbirth. Ten to twenty result in miscarriage.

No, we were not alone in our experience, yet at the time little about the subject was openly discussed. We had no one who'd been through a similar experience—no one to share our pain.

As for any future chances of having children, I came to my own conclusion that what happened with the triplets was an isolated incident. It would have no affect on future pregnancies. After all, I thought, it's pretty unusual to conceive triplets. If the doctor had known ahead of time that I was carrying three babies, maybe things would have turned out differently....

We recovered from the loss as best we knew how and were ready to move on. We felt a bit like a child who falls off a bicycle—getting back on is a little scary, but to get anywhere you have to overcome your fear and go on.

Little more than three months after I left the hospital, in late January 1976, I discovered I was pregnant again.

Phil and I wanted to believe the best for this pregnancy, but we responded differently this time around. I was somewhat reserved, and walked through the early months a bit soft-footedly. I didn't talk much with friends about the pregnancy. In fact, for months I didn't tell anyone I was pregnant. It was almost as if I was afraid to speak the good news too loudly.

Phil, on the other hand, was quite pleased with the news and shared it openly with friends. He felt God wouldn't allow something bad to happen again. "He knows the pain we both went through," Phil told friends. "God cares for us, and this pregnancy is his way of helping us go on with our lives. He knows our hearts' desire is to have children."

Phil was a bit more cautious, though, about my physical activity. When he was around, he was quick to come to my aid in lifting anything the least bit heavy.

When I told Lonnie the news, she was delighted for us. Now I felt more at ease when I'd visit her and her new baby. Yet her little girl was always a reminder of what our sons would have been doing by this time— cooing and smiling, being comforted by their mother's love.

Sometimes love hurts. And we were learning the cost of stepping out and trying again. But we were also being taught to believe the best and to trust.

Besides, now that I had felt the maternal bond between mother and child, I wanted to experience it again. Victor Hugo said, "Maternal love is a miraculous substance which God multiplies as he divides it."

This "miraculous substance" was now in me.

Late one May afternoon, as I walked around Freeville, I noticed a garage-sale sign and went over to check out the merchandise. Planted in the middle of the lawn was a big blue and silver baby carriage. It was bigger than life and seemed to tease me, daring me to buy it.

I stood there wavering back and forth.

It was a little too soon to take that step. *Not yet*, I thought.

I turned and walked home.

When I talked to my mom, she always cautioned me to take care of myself. Don't overdo it. Rest. Stop traveling. But I felt fine, physically.

My doctor assured me in my fifth month that everything was normal. I *was* confronted by gentle kicks almost every day now, and I was very noticeably with child.

When Phil went out of town for concerts, he always made sure there was someone to stay with me and that I was in good hands. I think he was afraid I would do too much when he was gone. Sometimes my caution got the best of me, making me leery of everything I ate, drank or did.

I guess a small part of me wondered if I was somehow at fault for losing the triplets.

By this time, our losses from the first pregnancy were rarely mentioned. Sympathetic listeners were hard to find. Friends assumed all was well, and we were already anticipating another child. Any secret fears Phil or I had we kept between us and seldom even voiced them to each other. We wanted to be an encouragement to each other.

As I entered my sixth month, I breathed a small sigh of relief. The doctors said full steam ahead. I finally allowed myself to get excited. I was going to be a mom!

Now I could walk through the baby department of a store and not cringe. Phil and I started talking seriously about names. We both loved *Ryan* if it was a boy, though a girl's name eluded us. I signed us up for a series of childbirth classes that would begin in September.

"Love Broke Through," Phil's second album, was finally recorded and released. The demand for concerts increased.

On the homefront, we relaxed about this baby, and knew it was time to start looking for a larger apartment. Something with two bedrooms and a yard would be great for our little family. When I was about six-and-a-half months along we discovered the perfect place—a huge, old farmhouse that had been converted into two apartments. We rented one immediately.

Our landlords were dairy farmers who went out of their way to help us get settled. They were happy to let us repaint the living room and kitchen. Upstairs, there was a large bedroom with a tiny room off of it that Phil could use for practicing his guitar or writing music. Down the hall was another medium-sized room, perfect for the baby. It had large windows that overlooked the backyard. I could already see a sandbox and a baby swing attached to the beautiful old maple tree. The room was painted baby blue so we decided to leave it, knowing it must be a sign of good things. Shelves lined one wall, and in my mind I pictured it filled with books and toys. A lovely wooden crib and changing table would just fit against the slanted ceilings. I reminded myself to start looking at garage sales for good used baby furniture.

We spent most of our days at the new apartment, getting it ready. I tackled the job of cleaning out the old refrigerator and oven. We felt confident and happy. Everything was going to be perfect.

One morning, five or six friends came over to help us paint. We laughed and talked of good times as the fresh paint slowly transformed the old farmhouse into our home.

We ended the night with four large pizzas, grateful for all our friends' help and support. By midnight Phil and I headed back to our old apartment, tired but happy. I crawled into bed, exhausted and glad to be off my feet. Phil reached over and patted my stomach, and the baby responded with several reassuring kicks.

As I drifted off to sleep, I felt myself sinking into a deep sense of peace and security that came from believing that God was about to bless us. I was tired, but my mind was still active. I made a mental list of all that needed to be done. Even though we were moving only ten minutes away, I had to box up all our things. With our neighbor's truck and a few cars, we could easily do the move. Our furnishings were sparse, but they were all we needed. I twisted and turned, trying to get comfortable. My back was aching from all the cleaning.

Finally, I fell asleep from sheer exhaustion.

The next morning I awoke slowly, feeling a bit stiff from all the activity the day before. Phil was still snoring as I maneuvered myself out of bed and shuffled into the kitchen to make some coffee. I felt a bit strange, as if the baby was shifting positions. My uterus felt hard as a rock, but there was no pain. I made myself a bowl of cereal and sat down at the kitchen table staring at my to-do list. It was only half crossed-off. *How am I going to move all these live plants?* I wondered. Plants were an inexpensive way of using up space in those days, and I had all shapes and sizes.

I began pulling them off the windowsills one by one and filling a huge cardboard box, trying to keep my mind off the fact that I wasn't feeling that great. As I climbed up to take down a hanging pot, my body felt like it was tied in a large knot.

I looked down to see Phil standing in the kitchen doorway. "What are you doing, standing up on that high stool?" he exclaimed.

For the rest of the morning, I orchestrated the action from a sitting position, as Phil did the packing. I felt tired and emotional. I was afraid to tell him—afraid to hear my own voice speak it—but my uterus was in a consistent rhythm of contractions.

"Are you all right? You don't look good," Phil said worriedly. "Why don't you go take a nap? I'll finish up in here."

Silently, I headed for the bedroom. *Maybe it'll help to lie down for awhile and sleep.* I dozed off for what seemed like an hour, only to be awakened by contractions accompanied with some pain.

"Phil, I think you'd better call the doctor," I moaned.

Once again, I saw that look of nervous frenzy, as Phil tried to compute what those words really meant. He set off quickly to dial the doctor's clinic. Five minutes later he was back in the room.

"He said to come into the office—*immediately.*"

It was late afternoon as Phil helped me out of the car. I thought, *This can't be happening again.* The twenty-minute drive had seemed like two hours, as the silence hung between us. I was afraid to voice my concerns until I saw the doctor, even though a million thoughts raced through my head. I fought to control myself as the contractions steadily increased.

When we arrived at the clinic, I could barely walk. The nurse knew I was coming and led me straight back to the examining room. Again, Phil had to wait in the lobby.

"You're dilating," the doctor said. "I'll call the hospital and tell them you're coming."

I don't want to go to the hospital, I thought. *I'm not ready to be there.*

During the agonizing drive, Phil broke the silence, "This can't happen a second time can it honey?"

I couldn't give him the affirmation he wanted to hear, as I stared into his pain-filled, questioning eyes.

While the nurses got me settled in my hospital room, Phil left to call some friends to tell them what was happening. I was hooked up to an I.V. as Dr. Bradford walked in and stood by my bedside, arms on hips. "We're putting in an alcohol I.V.," he said, assuring me this should slow down, and hopefully stop, the contractions.

I was at their mercy. I had to believe they knew what they were doing. I was willing to stand on my head and spit nickels if it meant saving this baby.

Instead, I endured twenty-four hours of living hell, as the medication took effect on my body. Phil sat by my bedside and prayed and read and slept. I went through phases of laughing, crying and sleeping, becoming incoherent as the medication consumed me. Then I got violently ill. It reminded me of the one and only time, as a young teenager, that on a dare, I drank a whole bottle of Boone's Farm wine.

Through waves of wild pain, I wondered how this was affecting my baby. On and off, I dozed into a restless sleep...only to be awakened by terrible, painful contractions.

A whole day passed.

Occasionally, Dr. Bradford came in and checked me. I could barely hear him, as he asked Phil to follow the nurse out of the room. The doctor then told the nurse to remove the I.V. and to prepare me for delivery.

Phil stopped by my bed and squeezed my hand. "This time I'll be with you," he whispered.

I was so doped up that the labor seemed like a frightful dream. A short time later, Ryan entered our world. Blue in color, he gasped for breath. He didn't cry, adding to the strangely quiet delivery room. I caught only a glimpse of him as the doctor checked his vital signs. I could also see the concern in the doctors' eyes as they quickly transferred my baby to a heated incubator.

"That's our son," Phil whispered in awe. "He's got to make it. He's a month further along than the triplets."

Ryan weighed in at two-and-a-half pounds.

The doctor looked at us both and said halfheartedly,

"This is a real fifty-fifty chance. Try not to get your hopes up."

Phil and I looked at each other. "Hope? What else is there?" said Phil.

Settled back in my hospital room with Phil at my side, I waited anxiously until the doctor came in. "We'd like to take the baby to the Perinatal Center in Syracuse, about an hour away," he said. "We don't have the equipment we need here to keep him going." Phil and I agreed at once.

Before they took Ryan away in the ambulance for the hour-long ride to Syracuse, a nurse brought him into my room. "I thought you might like to see him again," she said softly. By this time he was pink, and he looked beautiful.

I reached into the incubator and gently touched my son. I carefully stroked his dark hair. He looked so fragile as I traced his beautiful little ears with my fingers. I couldn't ignore how his chest moved violently with each breath. Wide-eyed, he looked at me as if to say, "I'm trying—for you, Mom."

Phil gently squeezed my arm and said, "It's time for him to go."

I watched helplessly as Phil and Ryan disappeared through the doorway. Phil would follow the ambulance to Syracuse.

A nurse came in and tried to be cheerful. "Ready for some rest?" she asked. I was definitely ready to sleep, to shut down my emotions for a few hours. I was too tired to think about what was ahead. My head fell back on the pillow, and I drifted off....

What seemed like only minutes later was really

hours. A baby's cry broke the quietness and jolted me awake. I turned my head to see a teenaged girl in the bed next to me, watching her newborn crying. She made no attempt to pick him up, though he obviously wanted to be held.

"I don't want to feed that baby, Mama," the girl said to the older woman at her bedside. "You do it."

I watched in amazement as the grandmother of this newborn held the baby and fed it a bottle. The baby's mother watched television and chewed gum, looking as if she'd rather be anywhere but here.

God, I don't understand, I prayed. *This young girl doesn't even want to cuddle her baby. She looks more inconvenienced than anything.*

Our son, whom I was aching to hold, was far away fighting for his life. Life was becoming more bewildering. My prayers came out as questions. *Why God? Why this time again? Why me?*

The next morning, when my roommate was released from the hospital, I was relieved.

Shortly after breakfast, Phil came in. He'd been in constant contact with the hospital about Ryan's condition. It was still a fifty-fifty chance that he'd pull through. His lungs were underdeveloped, but all two-and-a-half pounds of him struggled to survive.

Phil sat down on my bed and hugged and kissed me. "We've got to believe for the best. God can pull him through this," he said.

On the other hand, I couldn't allow myself to be too optimistic. I felt I was guarding my heart—but then, where did trust come in? I *wanted* to believe Ryan would pull through, but I knew it would be a long road if he did. How many times had I heard "All things are possible to those who believe?"

I knew my faith was being tested.

Phil sat on the corner of the bed, trying to encourage me. "All our friends are really pulling for us," he said. He looked weary, but I knew he wanted to drive up to Syracuse to see Ryan.

"Go ahead honey, I'll be okay," I said. "I need sleep today anyway. Go see your son," I said.

With that, he kissed me and left.

The rest of the day I slept, dozing fitfully as the nurses moved in and out. I tried to pray, but my thoughts were distracted by the sound of hungry babies being taken to their mothers for feeding. I felt left out, especially since the doctor never called to give me an update on our son. Maybe in a few days I would feel well enough to go see Ryan too.

That evening a friend stopped by. "We believe God's going to bring this baby through," she said confidently. "Phil sounded encouraged when he came by today."

"I hope so," I replied. "It's hard not being there to see him. I'm sick of this hospital. I can't wait to leave."

She went on, asking me whether I had faith to believe God could help Ryan. And suddenly, I just wanted her to leave. I knew she was kind to come, but her comments seemed so flippant. This was not her problem. It wasn't going to affect *her* life if Ryan lived or died. She already had a child, and I knew she couldn't relate to me.

With my eyelids getting heavy and with a few yawns, I guess I gave her the message—time to go. I lay back, feeling agitated. Again, I fell into a restless sleep.

The next day, Phil called me early. He was going to see Ryan first, then he'd come by and give me a report on his condition.

By early afternoon, I was anxious to know what was going on. Phil entered the room smiling. "I touched him, honey," he said. "He grabbed hold of my finger and squeezed it." Phil's eyes flashed with hope.

I managed a smile. I felt a little jealous, and I was aching to hold the baby.

We sat and chatted together; mostly about the apartment and nothing of consequence. We hadn't moved all our things yet, but Phil was working on it with some friends. I felt helpless in that area too.

I've got a dinner invitation from the Nichols, so I'm going to leave now," Phil said at last. "I'll come by in the morning. I love you," he said.

The nurse arrived with a tray of "gourmet cuisine." I picked at it, then pushed it aside. My thoughts were racing in a million directions.

What's really going on with my son? What if Phil's not telling me everything? The doctor said I could leave the hospital tomorrow.

I felt out of touch with everything and everybody....

Less than an hour later, Phil cautiously came back into my room. I was surprised to see him again, and I caught his eyes. He couldn't speak it, but I knew what he was going to say.

"*No, not my baby!*" I shouted.

Phil held me tightly and confirmed my worst fears. Ryan had died less than an hour before. He had developed hyaline membrane disease, and his lungs had ceased to function.

"My son, my son," I sobbed. "I love you. I'll always be your mother. It's not fair. This can't be happening again. I want my baby!"

Phil and I held each other and wept.

Then the nurse came in and gave me a sedative to drown out the pain.

But how could it?

Carrying all our questions with us

Monday morning, while I prepared to leave the hospital, Phil talked with the funeral director. The service was set for Wednesday evening. We would have a small service at the chapel in the local cemetery.

Because I couldn't bear to call my mom and dad again, I left that to Phil. I felt I was in a deep fog, looking for the door that led out to warmth and shelter. God seemed far away. I couldn't even pray, as my anger and rage got the best of me.

Phil arranged for us to stay with our friends, the Neilsons, who lived up in the hills, for a few days until the house was organized. When he drove me home to our new apartment to pick up a few things, we were greeted—carefully—by two dear friends, Glorya and Linda. "We're still moving your things in, so everything's not quite in order," Linda said apologetically.

I sank down into a chair at the bottom of the stairs while my two friends packed what I needed for the week. I looked around the apartment that we'd been so excitedly preparing for our "family." Normally, I would have been anxious about someone else setting up my entire house, putting things away where they thought they should go, but now I didn't care. In fact, it didn't matter if I ever came back there at all.

"Will you need these?" Glorya gently repeated. Her voice brought me back to reality. I nodded silently. When I looked into my friends' eyes, I could tell they ached for us. They knew how we'd anticipated this baby.

For the next week, Phil and I stayed with the Neilsons. Donna, a nurse, and Eric, a builder, opened their home to us. It was comforting as I took refuge in their guest room and cocooned myself under a beautiful old quilt and comforter.

Something was happening to me. I knew it. I could feel it. I wanted to escape. *World, go on without me—I'm checking out,* I thought.

Sleep seemed to repair my shattered emotions, and I slept as much as possible. Later, I understood that sleep was a gift from God.

I didn't want to touch with a waking mind the painful thoughts that tormented me.

When Wednesday evening arrived, I put on a long, burgundy flowered dress that I'd worn when I was pregnant. This time, though, I placed the belt back around my shrunken midriff and pulled it tight.

The rain was a cold mist as we headed for the funeral chapel. I knew in my heart that I was not prepared for this.

A handful of our closest friends were already there waiting quietly for us. I looked around to see Ted and Dawn Sandquist, the Harringtons, Linda and Stuart Scadron-Wattles, Scott and Nedra Ross, Bill and

Glorya, the Nichols, the Christiansons and the Neilsons. They all stood like statues waiting for us to make the first move. Few hugs were exchanged.

My eyes scanned the faintly-lit stone chapel. It was so cold in there. We were led to the small casket on a table, with two candlesticks dimly burning on each side. I could hardly bear to look at it. Could my son's small, frail body really be in there?

Scott Ross read a few words from the Psalms, and spoke briefly—stiffly, I thought. My ears were not hearing much anyway. In the tense, quiet atmosphere, I could feel the pulse in my neck. Phil was squeezing my hand so tightly the blood rushed out of it, making me feel flushed all over. But that was all I could feel.

My mind refused to connect with my heart. I would not let any of this touch me. I still couldn't believe this was happening to us.

When we sang a few of Ted's worship songs, I made a meager attempt to join in, mouthing the words. But my mind and heart were far away. I fought to hold back my tears, for fear I couldn't stop them once they started.

One of our dear friends, Bill Clark, read aloud a poem that he'd written about Ryan. Later, we inscribed his words on Ryan's tombstone:

> *Waiting for this son,*
> *we've yearned, we've learned he's with Someone*

...with Someone. With the Lord, that's what it meant, of course.

But why? Why not with *me*? I wanted my son. I wanted all of my sons.

I felt a confused mixture of hope and anger. I didn't cry for Ryan; I knew he was safe and in no pain. He would bypass many of life's struggles—but we would miss the joy of helping him through them.

As everyone left the chapel, Phil and I stood alone for a few last moments...with Ryan.

Peace to you, my son, I thought. At my side, Phil was doing his best to be strong for me, but I knew his heart was turned inside out. This was his fourth son, a son he was privileged to know only a few days. Gone were the dreams of singing him to sleep at night, or teaching him his first words. Would he have grown up to look like his papa, or carried on his legacy of music? We would never know.

We left arm in arm, carrying all our questions with us. And all our tears.

After the funeral, all of us gathered at the Neilson's home. When Phil and I walked in, I joined several women who were in the kitchen preparing food. As they worked, they laughed and caught up on news. I tried to act as if everything was okay.

My lip quivering, I went through the motions of communication. But my stomach was in a sickening knot. Donna asked me what I'd like to drink, but I could hardly hear her. Her voice was far away. I could feel perspiration trickling down my back. My legs felt like they were going to buckle underneath me, and I quickly headed for a chair.

Then the room began closing in on me. *I don't want to be here, with all of these people.* My chest felt tight as I tried to take a couple of deep breaths. I could hear talking and laughing in the background, as I looked desperately for a way to escape.

I was starting to panic. *I can't handle this. Where's Phil?* I scanned the room, and saw him talking with Ted.

I headed for the bathroom and locked the door behind me. Leaning against the wall, I slowly sank to the floor and sobbed. I had kept up a good front long enough. Now I didn't care. *God, where are you? I'm in pain. My heart is breaking...*

I wanted to scream and let my emotions out, but I was afraid nobody would understand. I was afraid to let these good friends know that I wasn't handling this well—that I had lost perspective and that I wasn't in control any longer.

I would have stayed in there until the last person left, but Donna kept knocking on the door checking on me. "Are you okay?" she asked.

"Yes, I'm fine," I lied.

Then I heard Phil's voice at the door, and I let him in.

"I'm so sorry this happened, honey," he said. His eyes welled up with tears when he saw my sorry state. He wrapped his arms around me and tried to give me whatever small measure of comfort he had left.

When we came out, he led me to the bedroom without much notice. Then he went back out to thank everyone and to say goodbye.

I crawled into bed and stared at the colored quilts that hung on the walls—red, yellow, bright calico. My heart was gray and dead. Despair filled the vacuum in my heart, along with anger and indifference. Everyone else was going home to their families and going on with their lives. I cried for myself and Phil. Where was our life going?

Phil soon came into the room and curled up on the bed with me. "I don't know why this has happened," he said. "Someday we'll know the answers to all our questions."

So you say, I thought.

The idealism with which we approached life was losing its shape. If God heard our prayers, then why didn't he always answer them? Putting ourselves in God's hands meant he would keep us safe, that nothing could go wrong. But it had *all* gone wrong. Was there somehow a purpose behind all this pain? I struggled, not knowing what to believe. I'd given God my life...my heart. Why was he intent on crushing it?

After a week at the Neilson's, we went home to our new apartment in Dryden. Our friends had done a wonderful job of getting things ready for us. There were fresh daisies on the kitchen table. I could smell one of Linda's wonderful asparagus quiches cooking in the oven. I knew it was her way of saying, "We love you."

During the next few months, Phil and I did our best to put our lives back in order. He traveled with his band doing concerts, and worked on songs for a new album when he was home. The band members—Lynn Nichols, Terry Anderson, Don Cunningham and Phil Madeira—rallied around him and gave Phil much-needed love and support, particularly when he was on the road.

Being able to express himself emotionally through his music also was healing for Phil. He had put "Ryan's Song" to music, and whenever he played it in concert, inevitably he'd meet others who had lost children. He was beginning to see how God was using our experiences to help others realize they weren't alone. His idealistic "peace-love-joy" view of Christianity began to change shape.

Phil groped to hold onto the comfortable, old way of thinking—looking for assurances that if we prayed and believed, things would always turn out right. That old way of thinking was failing fast.

Wanting to escape any way we could, we hung out often with friends and watched old movies. Anything to avoid the truth that pain and suffering were part of the larger picture of our lives.

We began to shut down emotionally with each other. We had trusted that this time all would work out, and we had been trampled on—worse than the first time. Our relationship became stifled. We didn't know how to help each other anymore.

Phil and I both struggled to find our own outside sources of comfort, and other people to help satisfy the void.

How I would have loved to sit down with someone who had gone through something similar—someone who could understand my feelings. If only I could have talked to a counselor and poured out my pain—without worrying whether he or she thought I was spiritual enough. I put up a great front around friends, so it was no wonder that everyone thought I was fine. I felt like no one had experienced such grief or loss themselves...After all, they were concentrating on life and living, not death and pain.

But the fact remained: It hurt that no one sought me out when I most needed it.

Many nights when I'd finally fall asleep, I would have the same nightmare. *I'm lying in the middle of this cold, sterile delivery room. Phil's by my side, smiling as we wait for the nurse to hand me our newborn son. "Here he is, Mrs. Keaggy, and he's beautiful!" the nurse exclaims. My hands reach out for him, all cuddled in the blue blanket. She stops suddenly. "Oh, there's been a mistake. Your baby's dead." She starts laughing hideously.*

"My baby," I cry. "I want my baby."

"Darling, I have to go now, I'm late for a concert," Phil says, patting my hand. "You'll feel better tomorrow...."

Then I'd wake up both Phil and myself, screaming

for them to bring my baby back. I'd be sobbing and soaked in sweat.

Phil would hold me and comfort me until I fell asleep.

We were also stuck, in a way. He was committed to a concert tour schedule—something that provided our income. But he found it terribly difficult to go on the road knowing that some nights I would have those dreams alone. And I did. I accepted that traveling was a part of Phil's job and always would be—but I was jealous that Phil had something he could pour himself into to escape.

In the coming weeks, people tried various forms of encouragement, none of which sat very well with me. One day in the grocery store, I ran into Marie in the cereal aisle, trying unsuccessfully to appease her two-year-old.

"Bernadette, how are you? Boy, kids can really be a pain sometimes," she said. "You'll know what I mean when you have them."

I forced a smile and quickly moved on. She had just added another stone to the wall around my heart.

On another occasion, after church, Nancy and Bob excitedly showed us their newborn baby, Zac. Nancy chirped as she plopped him in my arms that she was sure it would comfort me "since you never really got to hold your son."

My hands felt weak and clammy, and it was all I could do to keep from dropping him.

People offered us trite phrases like "I guess it's not so bad when you know your children are in heaven. That's comforting isn't it?" But I was not ready to be comforted by such shallow words. It was like jumping to point C before you understood fully what points A and B were all about.

I became more angry. I felt cynical and far away from God. *How could a loving God allow this? I thought he loved me.* I felt worthless and incapable.

When another well-meaning friend said, "I know God has a special plan in this for you and Phil," tears welled up in my eyes. *What plan? I thought children were a part of his plan.*

My anger troubled me, as my unanswered questions continued walling off my heart. A wall was growing between Phil and me, too. I was too caught up in my own pain to realize Phil was agonizing as well.

In *Disappointment with God,* Philip Yancey wrote, "True atheists do not feel disappointed in God. They expect nothing and receive nothing. But those who commit their lives to God, no matter what, instinctively expect something in return. Are those expectations wrong?"

All I knew was that I had trusted God with my dreams—I had trusted Phil and other Christians too. And I had been crushed.

Friends along the way

Life went on, with or without me. I found that either you run alongside your life, or travel behind with your feet dragging in the dirt. I was in the second category at this point.

Phil stayed busy. He traveled with the band for several days at a time, sometimes longer. I didn't go with him much, as he had quite an entourage with him. When the band was home, they'd rehearse new material in the small studio that had been built in the barn. Phil also helped Ted Sandquist put together a worship album of his songs. Besides the music, there was the dance company that Ted's wife, Dawn, had established, and a theater troupe run by Stuart and Linda Scadron-Wattles. Love Inn had become quite a creative, artistic environment.

Slowly, I forced myself back into the swing of things. Once again, we began to host the many single people in the community. And I enjoyed cooking for them and discussing life with them—as long as it didn't get too personal.

One evening, Phil Madeira, our friend and a member of Phil's band, stopped by. "I brought you a book," he said to me. "It's *A Severe Mercy*, by Sheldon Vanauken. It's also got some letters in it by C. S. Lewis."

I thanked him and set the book aside. I would look at it later. *It might be interesting*, I thought. Phil was especially curious about the letters from Lewis.

The following weekend, when the band left for three concerts in the midwest, I decided to tuck myself away and take a closer look at this book. As I skimmed the back cover, I read that after the painful death of his wife, Davy, Vanauken wrote to Lewis in hopes of gaining some understanding of his grief. Lewis had just lost his wife, Joy, to cancer, and the book contained seventeen of Lewis's letters, dealing with grief, loss and questions of faith. I was hardly into the first chapter before I was hooked.

Vanauken described the idyllic way he met Davy, and their wonderful courtship. They called their oneness "The Shining Barrier," which they felt nothing could penetrate. Immediately, I related to their story—it was so similar to the way Phil and I met, our courtship, our true friendship and the deep, abiding love we had for one another. And yet, for each of us—Lewis, Vanauken, Phil and me—pain had penetrated the barrier of human love and joy. Lewis's late-found love was cut short when cancer took Joy's life. I cried as I read his letters to Vanauken, sharing his honest feelings on grief and love.

Lewis wrote to Vanauken,

I am sure it is never sadness—a proper, straight, natural response to loss—that does people harm, but all the other things, all the resentment, dismay, doubt and self-pity with which it is complicated. (p.184)

I related to that wholeheartedly. It was true that nothing and no one in my Christian experience encouraged me by acknowledging that my sadness was normal. But on the other hand, my sorrow was all bound up with other, more destructive responses, like resentment and doubt.

Lewis went on to say,

Some people run away from grief, go on world cruises or move to another town. But they do not escape, I think. The memories, unbidden, spring into their minds, scattered perhaps over the years. There is, maybe, something to be said for facing them all deliberately and straight away. (p. 196)

Again, he had put his finger on the right issue. I had been thinking it would be easier to check-out—physically and emotionally—in my relationship with Phil. And here was Lewis, challenging me to see that this was perhaps the worst response in the long run. To face my grief "deliberately and straight away"—was I brave enough to do that?

For his part, Vanauken's honesty was also deeply freeing and refreshing. There was no pretense or denial. Grief, he said reflectively, is also a form of love. He spoke of it as ". . . the longing for the dear face, the warm hand. While it lasts, grief is a shield against the void" (p. 182).

These words brought up that old issue for me of self-protection. That tendency to build strong, inner walls—as if I could protect myself against all harm, as if I could keep my dreams and hopes and longing safe within me, until I could make them real.

And what motivated me the most, I think, was Lewis's encouragement to "patiently bear sorrow" (p. 190).

If I walked through this door of sorrow, which had obviously been opened up before me, what would I stand to lose? And what would I find on the other side? This was as scary as it was lifegiving. I was not stuck, I could choose to go on, with the hope of walking out of my inner pain in some way, at some point.

I was compelled to read on. I wanted to see what he did with his pain, how he handled it. I knew exactly what he meant when he spoke of the rage he felt, and the questions he shot up at the silent heavens. He openly expressed what I'd only dared to think.

One thing helped me immediately: Lewis assured Vanauken that grieving was a natural process that could easily take a year or so to work through. He counseled Vanauken not to ignore this grieving, so that healing could follow.

As I read these words, I felt as if a load had been lifted from my shoulders. Grief was normal. What I was feeling was *normal*. So it was okay to cry, to feel sad. It didn't make me any less a spiritual person. I had been striving to live up to a perfect or near-perfect image of "a true Christian." With Lewis's wise counsel, I realized that God loved me and accepted me with all my baggage. There was nothing I could feel or express that would make him stop loving me. How I had needed to understand that unconditional love.

I cried through almost every chapter of the book, as my pent-up emotions let loose. I carefully closed the book after the final chapter. I couldn't wait to share this with Phil.

The following week Phil and I read the book aloud together. It affected Phil deeply as well, and it gave us an opening to discuss our marriage and to talk about where to go from here.

Phil and I had to face the honest fact that we were basically non-confronters. We both had a way of holding in our negative thoughts and anxieties, hoping they'll go away. In reading the Vanaukens' story and how their love was tested, we realized that we had to face our pain honestly together. We had to accept the fact that pain and loss were changing our lives and marriage. It could destroy us—or it could make us stronger.

Phil and I turned to the Scriptures again, too. We read in Romans,

> The creation waits in eager expectation for the sons of God to be revealed. For the creation was subjected to frustration, not by its own choice, but by the will of the one who subjected it, in hope that the creation itself will be liberated . . . We know that the whole creation has been groaning as in the pains of childbirth right up to the present time." (Romans 8:19–20, 22)

These verses broadened my perspective of what it means to live in a world of pain and disappointment. We were not exempt from life's frailties. We had the choice to embrace our experiences and use them to benefit others, and to learn about life from an eternal standpoint.

We talked about the way tragedy helps us find out what we are really made of—when the essence of what we believe is shaken. It was a bit like God allowing Satan to test Job, time and again. He shook him to the core of his being, to see if he would still stand and trust God.

I saw that I needed work on that.

There was still the issue of our relationship. The fact that I felt myself growing apart from my friend and husband. I could tell that Phil felt the distance too. But at least we'd found some common ground where we could meet again—our hurt, and the desire to hold on to some bit of our faith, however small that was for me at the moment.

Our friends all had different ways of expressing their love and concern. All were welcomed, each in their own way. Some were deeply touching.

Elinor Hail called one day and asked if she could stop by. She was a music major at Syracuse University, and she and Phil Madeira were engaged to be married the following year. As we got to know Elinor better, we discovered that she knew all too well what it meant to lose a loved one.

Elinor was the youngest of four children. Her mother was a gifted artist who painted portraits in oils. Elinor told us, though, about the mood swings the rest of the family endured—fits of anger, frustration and depression that led her mother in and out of hospitals.

One Christmas in particular, when Elinor was ten years old, her mother lost control again and spent the entire holiday in the hospital, leaving a gloomy family at home trying to celebrate.

That following spring, as Elinor came home from school one day, she called for her mother, but heard no answer. As she walked from room to room, she smelled a strange odor. Opening the door to the garage, she found her mom lying on the floor, suffocated by carbon monoxide.

Elinor was devastated.

After the funeral, no one spoke again of her mother or the way she died.

Elinor spent most of her junior-high and high-school years suffering from rejection and low self-esteem. *Why did she leave us?* she wondered. *Weren't we worth living for?*

One of her mother's favorite songs was Handel's "Come Unto Me," and it was Elinor's favorite as well. Listening to that song gave her a sense of closeness to God long before she became a Christian. Several years later, through her husband-to-be, Phil, Elinor came to know Christ.

"I found comfort and healing from those painful wounds when I met Christ and gave him all the pain I'd been carrying," she told us. "Not that it evaporated instantly—but I knew that I no longer had to carry that terrible weight alone. He was there, and when I turned to him I felt his comfort."

I listened intently. In my anger and hurt, had I been turning to God—or turning away from him?

"Of course, I wondered sometimes," Elinor continued, "why God didn't some way prevent Mom's death. I suppose he could have, because he's God. But I'll never know the answer to that, not in this life anyway. And I found that if I focused only on my loss, I was in danger of missing all the other things that God was doing in my family's lives."

Shortly after Elinor became a Christian, she met a woman who had lived in her family's home as a college student. When Elinor talked about her newfound faith, the woman brightened. "Oh, I prayed for your family many hours while I was in your home," she said. "And look at how God answered those prayers." The woman must have been beaming when Elinor told her that her brothers had also become Christians in the years that followed.

The story made me think. *While I'm holding on to this pain—and shutting myself off from God—what am I miss-*

ing? What does he want to do in me that I'll lose if I don't learn to trust him more?

Then Elinor took out her guitar and played a song for us. I know it came from her heart, because the words moved Phil and me deeply:

Carry your sorrow no longer
Give Him your burden to bear.
How we all long to dwell with Him
Now your child is already there.

And He says, "All you who are heavy laden
Oh, I will give you rest.
And I will lift you up
And you shall endure the test."

He mourns for the sheep who have lost their way
He weeps for those who have strayed.
He cries for all who are weary and old
But He rejoices when His children come home to stay.

Carry your sorrow no longer
Give Him your burden to bear.
He's holding His child in His bosom
Remember He is love and He cares.

Thank you, Elinor, I thought. I'd forgotten.

The more Phil and I discussed our experiences with others, the more we became convinced that we live in a pain-filled, fallen world. Any idea that we can, that we *should* live an ideal life is a joke, a delusion.

I'd been pretty self-involved, thinking I was somehow specially singled out for disappointment. But pain and sadness were all around us, and I realized that every human being has a story to tell. Why had I been so blind to it before? It had taken Lewis and Vanauken—and Elinor—to make me realize that.

I felt my spirituality becoming more humanized, more *real* than I'd ever experienced before. It seemed to embrace all of life, all the human experience that lay between life and death.

And maybe, I thought, I could open the door to my soul again—just a crack—and venture out of myself once more.

My body will survive—
my heart is another story

Ted Sandquist, our pastor, called one day to tell me about a woman who had prematurely given birth to twins. They were alive, but in critical condition. He asked if I'd go visit the woman.

I thought about a Scripture I'd just read, where Paul says,

> Praise be to the God and Father of our Lord Jesus Christ, the Father of compassion and the God of all comfort, who comforts us in all our troubles, so that we can comfort those in any trouble with the comfort we ourselves have received from God. (2 Corinthians 1:3–4)

Hesitantly, I agreed.

All the way to the hospital, I talked to myself: *Put aside your own grief and try to comfort this woman. You know what she's feeling. Her babies are fighting for their lives. She needs you.* By the time I got there, I felt more at peace, sensing this was a mission from God, and that I could help this young mother.

As I walked into her hospital room, I felt her uneasiness. Smiling, I tried to offer words of encouragement. "I'm available anytime if you need me," I said.

She looked me straight in the eye and said, "Things are going to work out fine for me. God is going to allow both my children to live. I believe it." Her words hit me like a slap in the face. Her message was clear: *I don't need your sympathy. Your experiences don't relate to me. God will take care of this the way I want him to.* She seemed certain she had enough faith to solve her crisis.

I quickly retreated from the room. All the way home, I felt stung by her rejection.

On one hand, I knew why she had slammed the door on me and my offer of consolation. No doubt, she did not want to open herself to the possibility that her two babies might die, or to the overwhelming pain and despair that I must have represented to her. On the other hand, her rejection left me feeling confused and insecure. What about all the "good" I thought I was doing by visiting her? How was this giving comfort, as the Scripture promised? She didn't even *want* comforting.

When it came right down to it, when I was honest with myself, I really didn't have anything to say to her. Why had I gone? Because Ted asked me? You need to be able to help someone find God's presence when they are hurting—but had *I* been able to find him again?

In a few weeks, I heard that her babies had gotten through the critical stage. I was happy for her, and a bit jealous.

Phil and I decided it might be helpful to put some of my creative energies into art classes. Art always was a love of mine. Linda Christianson enrolled in some non-credit classes at Cornell University, and I joined her. I was happy to discover a new outlet, especially a creative one, to pour my energies into—to feel like I was doing something, creating something. To feel I was worthwhile, that I was important to God, to my friends and to myself. I realized I had been struggling to believe it.

Linda and I had great fun working on the potter's wheel and making copper and pewter jewelry. As I worked, I realized I was like this lump of clay in front of me. God was trying to mold me into something useful, beautiful. But I knew I was resisting the constant trickle of water he was adding to soften and shape me. Instead of opening myself to God, I was fighting—and as a result, I'd wound up feeling like a failure. *Maybe,* I thought, *it's time to stop resisting. Maybe Elinor was right...maybe I need to go to God for healing before this pain can be changed into something useful.*

Failure had done miserable things to my mind and self-image. In my own mind, I had failed again. Now I needed to go to God, the way I used to go to my own father, and to realize that he loved me no matter what I accomplished or didn't accomplish in this life. But all my emotions were holding me back—guilt, failure, anger—the voice inside that said, *I'm not good enough.*

Was I ready for God to reshape me? I wasn't sure.

One of the questions that haunted me was whether there was something physically wrong with me that kept me from carrying a child to term. I never returned to that local clinic, but instead sought out a doctor who dealt with difficult pregnancies like mine. I'd determined to have some tests run before I stepped into pregnancy again.

Several months later, I met Dr. Harris, who specialized in high-risk pregnancies at the Perinatal Center in

Syracuse, where Ryan had been hospitalized. He was knowledgeable and understanding, and he studied my health history while I filled in the details for him. Over the course of several weeks, he scheduled all sorts of tests, trying to rule out things such as a misshapen uterus, hormone problems or blocked fallopian tubes. I felt I was on a quest, determined to find out anything that may have caused my premature labors, so I was willing to withstand all the pricks, probes and highly uncomfortable tests to find out.

When the results were in, I anxiously made an appointment to talk with Dr. Harris.

"We've learned that several things are affecting your ability to remain pregnant," he said, "but I believe we can remedy these. For one, your progesterone level should remain high until you're ready to deliver. Yours is dropping down in your fifth and sixth month. We can give you hormone shots from about four months onward, on a weekly basis, to keep this level stable." I listened intently.

"You also have what is known as an incompetent cervix," he said. I had never heard of such a thing, but Dr. Harris went on to explain, "Your cervix is weak. Once the baby starts gaining considerable weight, your cervix starts dilating and proceeds into premature labor. Unfortunately, doctors can't really diagnose this until they spot a pattern of consistent premature labor, as in your case. We can remedy this problem by a delicate procedure in your fourth month of pregnancy. It's relatively simple, like having a purse-string pulled tightly around the cervix to keep it secure."

Surgery, I thought. *Now I'm getting nervous.*

"This only requires an overnight hospital stay," the

doctor was saying.

"Am I awake for this procedure?" I asked.

"Yes," the doctor answered, "but you're given a spinal block, or epidural, to deaden the pain. This surgery is not entirely without risk, however." I shifted around, trying to keep calm. "There is a chance that the procedure itself could actually cause you to miscarry. You have to weigh those risks."

I thanked him and told him I would let him know if and when I got pregnant again.

I drove back home, thinking over the things Dr. Harris proposed. Now I felt I had a tangible solution, that I'd accomplished what I set out to do. I was anxious to tell Phil when he returned from his concert dates. This doctor seemed to have a solution for my problem. It made sense to me. I was happy to have an option again—a sense of hope. But something inside me asked, *Is this what your hope is based on, Bernadette? On whether or not you can have children?*

A few months later, in January 1977, I found myself pregnant again for the third time. I immediately contacted Dr. Harris in Syracuse and made an appointment to see him. Phil and I went together to his office and discussed the proceedings. We had a game plan, and we were excited once again.

As the weeks passed, my old fears resurfaced, but I tried to keep them at bay with our newfound information. I wanted to be in control of the ride this time. I wanted to be a part of making this happen.

The doctor reassured me during my checkups, and confirmed the date he would perform the procedure in my fourth month. For my part, I walked cautiously week by week, careful not to overdo in any way.

Phil and I felt close again. We'd often take long drives along the Finger Lakes. All the grapevines were barren and dead-looking—it was hard to believe spring would bring them back to life again. "Phil," I said, "there's life within me again. It really could be different this time."

Phil squeezed my hand and responded, "The older we get, the frailer life seems to be. It's not so cut and dried any more—not so easy to take things for granted."

We stopped at one of our favorite views along the lake. You could see slight trickles of water through the frozen ice. Huge trees hung over the lake, looking spectacular in their coating of silver ice. It was quite a sight. We were both silent, pondering God's magnificent handiwork. There was something harsh and cold here, but beautiful too—God's presence was in the midst of it all.

In late April, almost four months into my third pregnancy, I awoke one morning with mild cramping. Keenly aware of anything out of the ordinary, I decided to call my doctor.

"Dr. Harris is out of town this week," the nurse said. "Dr. Raines is filling in." When I explained my symptoms, she told me to go to bed to see if the cramping slowed down. If not, Dr. Raines could see me that afternoon.

Hesitantly, I hung up and went to bed, hoping and praying the cramping would end. Suddenly, I felt weak and nervous. Phil checked on me repeatedly as he prepared to go out of town for a concert.

By early afternoon, the cramping intensified, accompanied by bleeding. Phil dropped what he was doing and drove me to the doctors' office in Syracuse.

It was a long, silent hour. Neither of us wanted to speak our worst fears again.

We waited for what seemed like forever for the doctor to arrive. I quietly made repeated trips to the bathroom, losing clots of blood. I wanted to scream out in pain and frustration, "Would somebody please help me here! I'm losing this baby!" But instead I painstakingly waddled into the examining room, waiting again for the doctor to show up. Phil sat with me, looking dumbfounded and helpless. By the time Dr. Raines came in, I was ill from the pain and heavy cramps and he confirmed what was already obvious to us. "Mrs. Keaggy," he said, "by the looks of things you've already lost this baby. You're going to need a D&C, to prevent infection and to make sure the uterus is clear. I'll make arrangements for you to be admitted to the hospital right away and schedule your surgery for today." I was in a daze as the nurse wheeled me out and explained things to Phil. We were in a numbed silence—no tears, simply trying to take in the disappointment as gracefully as possible.

After the nurse got me settled in a hospital room, the surgeon came in and introduced himself. He was an older man with graying hair, and he had an easy, kind manner. "This procedure will be painless," he said softly. "We'll give you general anesthesia and it will be over quickly." I thought, *My body will survive—it's used to pain now—but my heart is another story*. No one could do anything for the agonizing emotional ache I felt. There was no pill to lift my shroud of depression. The surgeon left Phil and me alone for about an hour until my surgery.

"How can I leave for the concert tonight with you going into surgery?" Phil asked. But we both felt Phil needed to honor his commitment and leave for New Jersey. I was so used to his touring that I thought I could handle this alone. Phil hugged me and reluctantly left the hospital to make arrangements for me to be picked up the next day by a friend.

I was alone that night in the hospital, alone with my thoughts. I also was afraid. I whispered to God, *"Are you there? Help me. I can't do this alone."* Then the nurse came in and wheeled me to surgery. The anesthesiologist started an I.V., and soon the clear liquid running into my vein blocked out any conscious thoughts. I awoke in yet another recovery room, thinking, *It's over and that is that*. Confusing thoughts filtered through my mind: *I can't even sustain a pregnancy long enough for the doctor to help me. I'm a failure*. I was tired of trying to figure out God, and my own life, for that matter. I just wanted to sleep.

The next morning a friend picked me up from the hospital and took me home with her for a couple of days, until Phil returned. Phil called often, anxiously checking on my condition. After a couple of days of being in that busy household, surrounded by children, I insisted I was well enough to go home.

That's when I hit bottom. I felt defeated. I had no more strength to fight. I was through with running this emotional and physical race. I cried out, "I give up. The ball's in your court, God. The set is over."

I went through the motions of each day. It was a struggle even to get out of bed. I had a hard time finding pleasure in anything. Cooking, which I loved, became a chore. It was depressingly cold and overcast outside, and I felt trapped and discontented. I tried reading Scripture, and that gave me some comfort. I reread the letters of C. S. Lewis, who said, "God, who foresaw your tribulation has especially armed you to go through it not without pain but without stain." Somehow I had to pick up my armor again and battle my way through this.

When Phil came home from the studio one day, we tried talking about our feelings. I told him I wanted to get out of the baby business. Would he join me? He agreed. We decided to put our dream of having children on the shelf—until we felt it time to pull it down and dust it off again. When I went back to see Dr. Harris for a check-up after surgery, I could tell he felt awful about what had happened. He wanted to help us, but I hadn't gone far enough in the pregnancy for him to do the procedures. "If and when you both feel it's right to try again, I'll be with you 100 percent," he said. I thanked him and left feeling that I was closing a chapter of my life.

During the following weeks, Phil and I tried to pick up the emotional pieces and go on. But we were numb; every part of our lives seemed strained. Phil and I each retreated into our separate worlds. Our communication faltered as both of us felt unable to give each other what we needed. Phil poured his energy into his music. But he was at a loss for words and so began expressing himself instrumentally, which eventually led to his album *Master and the Musician*. Sometimes music expresses our feelings in ways that words cannot. That's how Phil worked out his pain and confusion. But I could find no outlet for my grief. Not that I didn't try. I frantically filled the void with art and dance classes, and with cooking for friends—anything to help fill the emptiness that I began to believe was permanent. I even turned to soap operas for an escape. I'd plan my day around getting home in time to see "One Life to Live." The actors' problems seemed so constant and futile that it made me feel better about my own.

It was a difficult time in our marriage. Although we still loved each other, the years of emotional pain had strained our relationship. Our opinions on life were no longer the same—something that bothered Phil more than me. Phil was more accepting of what we'd been through, while I seriously questioned everything I believed about God. Losing his mother while still in his teens had both toughened Phil and mellowed him. He wasn't demanding answers to questions that, as far as he could see, would never be answered in this life.

Phil's faith seemed stronger than mine, and he believed all our pain would somehow work out for good. After all, the death of his mother brought him to his first spiritual awakening and changed his life radically. So I found myself searching for my own spiritual identity, apart from Phil—a good thing, but frightening, too.

At this time, we also began questioning some of the things our church taught. Some of their thoughts on discipleship and servanthood began tilting to the left. We had seen in our travels how much bigger God was than our little corner of the world. The reality of God's sovereign ways was finally getting through to me. My definition of faith also began to change.

Before my third pregnancy, I still believed I was in control of my future. If I did certain things right, I thought, the outcome would be as I planned. The Scripture, "In his heart a man plans his course, but the Lord determines his steps" (Proverbs 16:9), took on new meaning for me. For so long I had thought: *I'm healthy. I'm loving. There's no reason I should be denied the privilege of having a child.* When the doctor told me my physical problems could be treated, I thought there was no stopping us. It was humbling to realize that no matter how hard I tried, the result was in God's hands. I could not manipulate the outcome.

During the months ahead I began to realize that our faith does not mold God into what we want him to be. Our faith cannot force God to give us what we want, no matter how badly we want it. His mercy and love for us far outweigh what we may desire.

Settling some of these issues in my mind allowed me to once again look beyond myself and evaluate what was happening around me. I saw that Phil and I had started looking more to other people for strength, friendship and encouragement, instead of turning to one another. I enjoying my time with single friends more as an escape than anything else. Phil spent more time with his buddies in the band because I no longer listened to him or reached out to him. Our emotional oneness was gone, and I wanted it back.

One night, as Phil practiced his guitar in the small room off of our bedroom, I went to him. "We've got to talk," I said.

He looked up at me, his eyes filled with a painful, knowing look. "I know we do," he said as he set his guitar aside and made room for me next to him.

My heart pounded as I said what I had already rehearsed in my mind a number of times: "I'm sorry, honey, that I haven't been here for you as a wife or a friend."

"We always said we'd be honest with God, with ourselves and with each other," he quietly replied. "We've lost sight of that haven't we? I'm so sorry we've allowed all these experiences to separate us." We held each other and cried, each one asking the other for forgiveness for letting our own selfishness rule our lives. I felt the stony corners of my heart start to dissolve.

After that night, we started setting aside time together, away from the house, where we could have each other's undivided attention.

Our relationship was maturing. We decided it was okay to have differing opinions, that it was actually healthy and helped us make better decisions together. We were confident enough in each other's love to respect each other's individuality. We felt that even if we never had children—a good possibility—we were important enough to God and to each other to continually work on our marriage.

8

" I will make darkness into light..."

And so in the summer of 1977, Phil and I not only returned to the basics in our relationship, but we also saw it deepen. We came to see there were choices to be made about our lives, and that we were the only ones who could make them.

For one thing, the leaders of the Love Inn fellowship had made quite a few decisions about Phil's career—his traveling and recording. That had been okay while he first started on his solo career. Now he and I began to make more decisions on our own, rather than letting others in the church assume that responsibility. Doing so felt good and right, and I watched Phil develop new maturity in the process.

We also realized that we needed to gain some perspective on our grief. I was so caught up in the painful losses, and Phil was so preoccupied with his career. We needed to devote some time to taking a hard look at our lives. This in itself was a fight—my tendency after each loss was to pull into myself. When I did, real, ongoing communication between Phil and me died. We knew we were going to have to fight for our marriage, against all the emotional trauma that had separated us. At the bottom of it all, we had to battle this together.

Here were facts we had to face: Phil and I did not share enough of our everyday lives together. The date-nights we had were good—but when we went out together, we seemed not to have a lot of shared interests to talk about. We were living separate lives together.

We determined to find new shared pastimes to

rekindle our closeness and enthusiasm for being together. Phil enjoyed running, and had even run a marathon. I decided I could enter his world a little more by taking up jogging. He encouraged me to pull out my old running shoes and join him on his runs.

My first time out, I half-walked, half-ran a mile. Over the years of going in and out of pregnancies, I was always afraid to overtax my body. Now it felt good to push myself and to sweat.

Day after day, Phil patiently kept pace with me until finally I could run three miles with him. It felt good—and I began to realize the importance of physical exercise to my emotional well-being. I gained not only a sense of accomplishment but also found companionship, as Phil and I regularly jogged the beautiful trails around BB Lake near Cornell University. From time to time, we even recruited friends to join us. The physical benefit was that I was getting my battle-scarred body into shape for the first time in years. And at the ripe old age of twenty-two, it felt great!

More important, Phil and I desperately needed time away together. We needed some distance from our circumstances. We hadn't taken a real vacation since our honeymoon, and decided that a trip to Hawaii would provide the relaxation and space we needed—to rest, to think, just to *be*. We made plans and space on our calendar for twelve days in Hawaii. We felt a bit guilty about the extravagance—but not too much.

Just before our trip, while Phil was touring Texas with the band, several concert dates were cancelled due to unforeseen circumstances. Happy for the break, Phil made arrangements to fly home so we could have a few days together.

It was pitch-black, about five o'clock in the morning, as he caught a ride with a friend to the Dallas-Fort Worth Airport. As Phil and the driver chatted, Phil looked up to see something coming fast in their lane. *"No!"* he yelled.

The driver slammed on the brakes, but their car crashed into another vehicle stopped in the middle of the highway. Phil's head rammed the windshield, leaving him in a daze.

In an instant, several more cars came crashing into them. The driver hit his head as well, leaving him only semi-conscious.

Somehow Phil managed to steer the car into the grassy median, and got out through the side window. Shaking, he walked to the other cars to check on victims. People were injured and bleeding, but no one was killed. When the ambulances arrived, Phil was taken to the hospital to make sure he didn't have a concussion. Then he was released.

When Phil got home, I listened to his story and felt my knees get weak. "You know, Bernadette," he said, "through it all I kept thinking about how Mom died in that car crash. Today, I felt like it as easily could have been me.

Silently, I thanked God for his mercy in sparing Phil's life. I loved this man who had been through so much with me. I wondered if Phil really *knew* that—wondered if, in turning in on myself so often, I showed him the love I felt for him....

We must have looked pretty pathetic as we left for Hawaii. Phil sported a lovely black eye, and walked stiffly from muscle aches and bruises. We felt like two battle-scarred warriors heading for warm, peaceful shores. As the plane lifted off, I looked closely at Phil as he sat next to me. The hair at his temples was starting to gray. He was as thin and taut as ever—but the years of traveling and stress were showing in tiny lines around his eyes. Yes, I was still in love with this man. And I was grateful to have this time with him. *Life is so fragile, so much out of our control,* I thought.

Mornings in Hawaii, I combed the beaches for shells and sea life, taking in the warm tropical air. Phil took advantage of the extra hours of sleep to revive his aching body. At lunchtime, we'd go out and discover out-of-the-way restaurants together. Then we'd ride bikes past acres of sugarcane, and soak in the sun's rays on the sandy white beaches. I understood why people called this place paradise. Not only for its amazing beauty, but for what it does to you inside. I felt happy and free. No one knew us, and we could be ourselves without having to meet anyone's expectations. We made the most of each glorious day, laughing together and rediscovering our love for one another.

I thought about how dead-set I had been on controlling our future. I had insisted that God work within the goals I had set for my life.

Now I yearned for a simpler spirituality, one that allowed me to accept my frail humanity, my weaknesses and let God be God. I was tired of trying to live within a formulated Christianity that kept God in a box—a box controlled by me. It was so upside-down, really. Find your dream or goal; pray for it; *poof*—God, like a genie-in-a-bottle, gives you what you want. Where did God-our-Maker, God-the-Sovereign-One come in?

One of those clear-shining mornings, when I was alone on the beach with the ocean spread before me like eternity, I read this in Oswald Chambers's *My Utmost for His Highest*:

> ... sin, sorrow, and suffering *are*, and it is not for us to say that God has made a mistake allowing them. Sorrow removes a great deal of a person's shallowness, but it does not always make that person better. Suffering either gives me to myself, or it destroys me. You cannot find or receive yourself through success, because you lose your head over pride. And you cannot receive yourself through the monotony of daily life, because you give in to complaining. The only way to find yourself is in the fires of sorrow. Why it should be this way is immaterial. The fact is that it is true in the Scriptures and in human experience. You can always recognize who has been through the fires of sorrow and received himself, and you know that you can go to him in your moment of trouble and find that he has plenty of time for you. But if a person has not been through the fires of sorrow, he is apt to be contemptuous, having no respect or time for you, only turning you away.

Had I really seen myself in the fires of sorrow? Had I received myself yet, my true self, from God? Or was I still Bernadette Keaggy, made in the image I wanted her made in?

When Phil and I returned to New York, in many ways we were different people. We had crossed a threshold I could not exactly name. But our love for each other felt freer, less weighed down by expectations and demands. The same was true of our love for God. We were ready to stop *performing* for him, and simply to rest in his goodness, no matter what. We were not so intent on getting what we wanted, and a little more ready to let God carry us through whatever he might have for us—whether from our perspective it seemed good or bad.

On the practical side, we decided not to focus on having children for now. It wasn't easy, because our friends' families were growing. Almost everywhere we went, we saw children laughing, crying, clinging to their mothers' knees. That pulled on our heartstrings, and we felt we were missing out. But we accepted that a family was not in God's plan for us right now.

When we got back to Freeville, we turned to friends who weren't preoccupied with children, and enjoyed hours of conversation and good food together. We began to meet one night a week to read a book aloud together, then discuss our thoughts on it. We also regularly met at Stuart and Linda's after church on Sunday night, along with two or three other couples, to watch episodes of *Masterpiece Theater* and visit. Simple acts like these bonded us with these friends for life.

I focused on another practical part of my life, which

I'd ignored until recently. I continued taking care of my body. When I did, my self-esteem rose, and my outlook on life grew more positive. Some days I'd run hard and long until I'd feel sweat pouring down my skin. Many days, I also felt my pent-up emotions rise to the surface, and I let go of them.

Still there were unexpected incidents that let me know some of the hurt remained.

One morning after a run, a friend and I sat in a little cafe near BB Lake, drinking coffee. Out of the blue she asked, "Do you feel you've gotten over the miscarriages? Do you plan to get pregnant again?"

It caught me off-guard, and the word *miscarriage* seared my emotions. Instantly, my heart started pounding and my blood pressure rose.

"Ellen," I said, composing myself, "my first two pregnancies were not miscarriages, which happen in the first trimester—they were premature births. When you go into labor and deliver a two-and-a-half-pound infant who lives for three days, that is *not* a miscarriage."

She was obviously embarrassed, and I backed off with a halfhearted smiled.

"I'm sorry," Ellen said. "I was just concerned about you. I didn't realize it was still such a touchy subject. You seem to be adjusting so well."

It was true. My emotions could still become volcanic at a moment's notice, and I'd find myself off-balance.

Healing is a slow, daily process, I learned, and there's no quick way out. I was glad for a friend like Ellen, who needed no facades, no apologies or explanations.

One day, Phil and I browsed at one of his favorite guitar shops in Ithaca. While Phil chatted about guitars and amps with Paul, the owner, I struck up a conversation with his wife, Ann, who was five months pregnant. Excitedly, she told me about the baby's movements and how much they were looking forward to their first child.

I kept the conversation light, and didn't offer any personal explanations of my own.

Several days later, I overheard Phil talking to Paul on the phone. He was offering condolences. When he got off the phone, he told me Ann had gone into premature labor and had lost the baby. I sat down as another unexpected wave of emotion came over me. I knew all too well the explosion of grief they were feeling.

The next day, I called Ann to let her know I was available to talk if she needed and to let her know we'd been through same grief. This time, I was more aware of her needs than my own, and I was careful not to overshadow her grief by talking too much about my own. I just let her talk and cry. From my heart, I empathized with her.

When I hung up the phone, I stared at Phil. Sure I'd read statistics, but they were devoid of the human element. "We're not the only ones going through this, are we?" I asked. "Ann and Paul probably feel the same way we did—that no one fully understands. We need to keep in touch with them and support them right now. They need to know somebody cares."

"Paul was so excited about having a boy," Phil said.

"He looked forward to buying him his first baseball glove and teaching him to ride a bike. I dreamt about those things too—buying my son his first guitar, writing songs together, singing him to sleep at night." Then he fell silent for a minute.

There was the question again, hanging silently in the air between us: *Why?* "It's difficult learning to trust God," he said, "when we don't have all the answers. Bernadette, I know someday there won't be sadness or pain or tears. That's our hope."

He spoke so so matter-of-factly—but so convincingly, because I knew he believed it.

After Hawaii and Ann's loss, I experienced something new. It seemed as if something was being exposed at the roots of my life—an emotion so deep it dictated much of my life. I became acutely aware how much *fear* influenced me.

For instance, when Phil was away traveling with the band, I constantly battled the anxiety of being alone. I often invited my friend Jacqueline Brown to come stay with me. I struggled with what I could control in my life and what I couldn't.

One night in particular, Phil was gone and I lay in bed, alone, listening to every noise my ears picked up.

For some reason, I became convinced someone was lurking around the house trying to find a way to get in. I was totally paralyzed by fear, as old memories flooded over me. Once, back in Ohio, the police arrested a young man who lived several houses down from ours, who was accused of raping a number of girls in our area. And I walked past his house every day on my way to school.

Now I saw that fear had woven itself into my life and was trying to paralyze me as I lay terrified in my bed. This was crazy! I felt angry at myself for being so controlled by my fears, angry enough to finally face it. I had built so many walls, trying to protect myself—but all I protected inside those walls was a fearful child, not the mature woman I wanted to become.

Suddenly, I was tired of it all. I cried out for God's peace and his assurance. I made a conscious decision: I would no longer be a prisoner in my own home—or a prisoner in my own heart. The words from Psalm 4:8 lulled me to sleep: "I will lie down and sleep in peace, for you alone, O Lord, make me dwell in safety."

Maybe I was finally ready to accept that God's safety was not the smooth-sailing kind I'd been looking for.

I found myself at the dangerous edge of a major choice—it seemed there was no way around it, like a chasm looming open at my feet, and the ground before me was crumbling. To go on with life, real life at a deep level, meant that I had to stay open to love. Without love, why be alive? But to love seemed to mean risking more loss and more hurt. Why did these two things have to be linked together? And I knew that to choose love and life gave me no mystical guarantees.

Our old "friend," C. S. Lewis, helped me once

again, when I discovered what he'd written about the risks of loving in his book, *The Four Loves.* "To love at all is to be vulnerable," Lewis warned. But to lock your heart away from love—as I was tempted to do, thinking I could keep myself safe from hurt—was far more dangerous according to Lewis. He nailed me directly in the soul when he wrote,

> . . . safe, dark, motionless, airless—[your heart] will change. It will not be broken; it will become unbreakable, impenetrable, irredeemable. The alternative to tragedy, or at least to the risk of tragedy, is damnation. The only place outside of Heaven where you can be perfectly safe from all the dangers and perturbations of love is Hell. (p. 169)

Was that what I wanted—to go on living in a "safe Hell" of my own making? Or would I risk again, become vulnerable, like clay in a potter's hands—maybe never be able to make my life the way I had always dreamed of it?

Lewis concluded, "If our hearts need to be broken, and if [God] chooses [the loss of someone we love] as the way in which they should break, so be it" (p. 170).

Yes, I was tired of the fearful old me. Maybe I would never completely lose my fears. But I was ready to admit that perhaps all the good things I tried to fortress my heart with—things that seemed good and joyful and of the light—were not the *ultimate* good, because they were not lasting. And maybe the events that I thought of as "dark" were just deep shakings to wake me up—love, of a totally different kind. *So be it.*

In any case, as I said, I felt as if there were no going

back from this edge. I wanted to, I had to, make a leap across this chasm that I'd come to in the floor of my soul.

In April 1979, Phil and I traveled to California while he worked on a new album with Buck Herring. I was happy to have a change of scenery for a couple of weeks. Buck and his wife, Annie, had become dear friends, and had repeatedly supported us emotionally and financially when the cost of Ryan's hospital care became overwhelming. They also lived in such a freedom in Christ, and we found that refreshing.

We stayed in California off and on over the next months, and our outlook continued to broaden. We began feeling that a move was in store for us, that our time in New York was over. We anxiously looked forward to a new chapter in our lives. And so as we traveled to various states that spring, we kept an open mind about where we would plant ourselves.

In June, while Phil played a concert in Kansas City, we spent some time with our friends Paul and Sharon Clark. We felt a strong connection there with a number of friends we had grown to love and appreciate over the years. And it was there we met Bruce and Nancy Coleman.

Bruce was a pastor at the church our friends attended. We were invited to their home for dinner one evening and, in the course of conversation, Bruce told us that he was diagnosed with Hodgkin's disease. For more than a decade he had lived on the edge of the disease, going in and out of remission. He and his family learned to live day by day, never knowing when the disease would recur. His faith was strong, and we were amazed how a man facing such personal trauma could reach out so lovingly to us.

When Bruce turned his comments to us and our painful experiences, we gave him our undivided attention. He said he believed God was going to give us children and bring a time of healing and grace into our lives. This was a man who seemed so near the heart of God that we didn't take his words lightly.

As Phil and I talked later about what Bruce said, we were amazed that someone so near death could speak such life-giving words to us.

And though I wasn't sure I was ready for it, something in my heart believed that Bruce's words were more than wishful thinking. I struggled with them—as if they were a test of all I'd been learning. Could I let go of fear, and just believe?

For his part, Phil wrote his heart's answer into a song, which he later recorded:

Last night I asked my heavenly Father
about the way I should go.
I said "Lord I can't see your path before me,
all I can see is rocky road.
So take me through."

And He spoke to me these words of simple truth:
"And I will lead the blind by the way they do not know,

In paths they do not know I will guide them.
I will make darkness into light before them,
and rugged places into plains.

These are the things I will do, I will do, I will do,
And I will not leave them undone.
These are the things I will do, I will do, I will do,
And I will not leave them undone."

Well, I'm only one of countless thousands,
who have walked along pilgrim's way.
And whenever I thirst, I'll seek my Lord first,
and listen to what He will say.
Lord, let me hear you!

And He spoke to me these words of simple truth:
"Behold I will do something new, now it will spring forth
and will you not be aware of it?"
I will even make a roadway in the wilderness,
and rivers in the desert.

These are the things I will do, I will do, I will do,
And I will not leave them undone,
These are the things I will do, I will do, I will do,
And I will not leave them undone."

"I will make darkness into light...."

I knew that only God could make that claim, and somehow these words seemed right and true for us.

Was it possible that the darkness was about to be turned, by God's power and grace, into a new-dawning light for us?

Trusting, no matter what

When we returned to New York, two major events occurred. First, we decided to move to Kansas City. It was difficult telling our friends we were leaving, but they understood it was time.

Second, I became pregnant.

This time it was no surprise, but a result of our conscious decision to try again. Two years had passed since my last pregnancy and motherhood was again tugging at me. With the right medical attention, we felt we had to give it one last try before we resorted to other options, such as adoption.

By now Phil and I had decided that sometimes you have to step out and trust God, no matter what. Not that the outcome is guaranteed to be wonderful. But we knew he would be there for us if we fell again. I now believed the outcome of this pregnancy was already determined—and certainly not by me.

We solidified our plan, and flew to Kansas City to look for a new home and to check out a good doctor. Within a week, we had found a lovely old stone house for sale, and the down payment matched Phil's royalties from Newsong records. I was ecstatic over owning our first home. My creative juices were already flowing, and I pictured the changes we would make after it was ours.

While we were in Kansas City, I also called the hospital connected with the local university and asked for recommendations on doctors. Several sources led me to Dr. Charles King, whose forte was dealing with high-risk pregnancies. I called and made an appointment to see him when we returned for good.

Within a matter of weeks, we were in our new home. We had not even unpacked, however, when we set off for New Zealand and Australia. Phil was scheduled to perform a couple of weeks of concerts and a music seminar, and I was along for the ride. I felt determined to not let this pregnancy, or my fears, keep me from joining Phil in this experience. The doctor couldn't do anything for me anyway until my fourth month, so if something happened sooner, I felt it was out of my control.

In New Zealand, we were welcomed by our gracious hosts David and Dale Garrett, who knew the meaning of true hospitality. They lavished us with loving care as we stayed in their home during the first week of our travels. Phil's concerts were well received, both in New Zealand and in Australia. The people appreciated Phil coming the distance from the United States, and we felt enriched by our time in these lovely countries.

And inside, I felt that something was different—truly different—about this pregnancy.

Upon returning to Kansas City, we went about the task of unpacking boxes that lined the rooms—and enjoyed it. With our friends' help, we tore up old orange shag carpeting and refinished the beautiful wood floors underneath. Phil scraped off layer upon layer of old wallpaper and I, quite contentedly, picked out a new pattern.

My belly started to bulge once again, and those

small first flutters of life became real and precious. It was once again a walk of trust for us, and we took it day by day. We came to appreciate the loving care and skill of Dr. King, as he cautiously monitored my pregnancy. When we made it to the surgery at the end of my fourth month, I felt relieved.

As Phil checked me into the hospital and got me settled in my room, I felt uneasy. The anesthesiologist came in to give me a spinal block, and I thought back to all my dreadful hospital experiences in the past four years. *Today's experience could be just as bad*, I thought. *This procedure could either help bring life, or cause me to miscarry.* But we were willing to take the chance, and I would not give in to fear.

Phil was by my side in surgery as Dr. King sewed a tiny purse-string suture around my cervix, then pulled it tightly closed. With only mild discomfort, I was back in my hospital room within the hour. These stitches would stay in until it was time to deliver.

Dr. King came into my room after surgery. "Everything went well," he said, "and we'll keep you overnight to make sure labor hasn't been induced. But the chances are slim. This procedure will bring on labor in about five percent of the cases—and hopefully you won't be one of them."

Yes, hopefully, I thought.

The next day I was released from the hospital. I was told to take it easy, but I was not confined to bed.

We'd crossed a major milestone, one step at a time. Inside, I let out a big cheer—but on the outside, a relaxed smile fit the occasion.

Phil tried to cut back on his traveling as the months rolled by. He wanted to be by my side as much as possible, to make sure I was following doctor's orders. On one of my weekly doctor visits for my hormone shot and check-up, Phil joined me. When I came out of the examining room, he was furiously writing down words to what soon became the song "Little Ones."

"You know, I was sitting here thinking about your conversation last week with your sister," he said. I had shown her pictures from the book, *The First Nine Months of Life,* pointing out what stage our baby was in. She was amazed that a three-month-old fetus had fingernails and could even suck its thumb.

"How many people don't realize that life begins at conception, not birth?" Phil said. "How many abortions take place because women aren't informed about what's going on inside of them when they become pregnant?"

The following week, he performed the song for the first time at a concert in San Bernadino, California, before an audience of about 8,000:

> *Who will speak up for the little ones,*
> *helpless and half-abandoned?*
> *They've got a right to choose*
> *life, they don't want to lose.*
> *I've got to speak up, won't you?*

Equal rights, equal time
for the unborn children.
Their precious lives are on the line.
how can we get rid of them?
Passing laws, passing out
bills and new amendments.
Pay the cost and turn about,
and face the young defendants.

Many come and many go,
conceived but not delivered.
The toll is astronomical—
oh, how can we be indifferent?
Little hands, little feet,
tears for him who made you.
Should all on earth forsake you now
yet he'll never forsake you.

Forming hearts, forming minds,
Quenched before awakened—
for so many deliberate crimes
the earth will soon be shaken.

When Phil finished, the audience rose to its feet with a roar. Until I gave birth to our first three sons at five-and-one-half months, I didn't fully understand the sad reality of abortion. It sickened and pained me now to think that doctors purposely kill babies in the womb, sometimes much further along in pregnancy than I was now. I believed that if women could see and touch a premature baby as I had touched mine there would be no choice but to give life, not take it.

Phil and I chuckled together as my silhouette grew huge. How could I stretch another inch?

Daily, I read from a book called *The Child Within*, by Mari Hanes. It discussed each month of pregnancy in the physical sense as well as the spiritual. I still had to battle some old fears and some new ones. *Surely, something was going to burst this bubble,* I thought. *Don't get too excited. What makes you think this will have a happy ending?* Daily I fought a battle with cynicism and fear, but deep down I wanted to believe God would give me this child.

As I passed my eighth month, I realized that this child had a good chance to make it. But what if something went wrong right at the last? I shared my fears with Phil, and he understood. We decided that God had brought us this far and he would give us the child he wanted us to have. There was that challenge again— *to trust completely, no matter what.*

In the wee hours of the morning, on March 19, 1980, I was awakened by annoying, consistent contractions. The baby wasn't due for three more weeks.

I decided around 5 a.m. to call Dr. King at home. He told us to meet him at the hospital by 6. We fumbled around the house, not quite prepared, and eventually made our way out the door to St. Joseph's Hospital.

We were greeted by Dr. King, waiting for us, all calm and smiling. It was comforting.

He examined me, and snipped the cervical stitches. Then I was in full labor.

Phil and I walked the halls, pacing back and forth. *How ironic,* I thought. *After all this time of holding on to this pregnancy, this baby is going to come when it's good and ready.*

We spent the next hours in nervous anticipation. We walked and talked until the contractions were close and hard. Was this child really going to be ours—to keep and raise? We could hardly wait to open this long-awaited package. Was it a boy or a girl? Who would it look like? The last stage of labor was long and slow, unlike the other pregnancies. Phil coached me through the breathing process and, as the pain grew more intense, I held onto him.

Our friends came in and out, cheering us on. At one point, I asked our good friend, Paul, to remove himself and his video camera from the room. I didn't want to have to look back and see myself sweating and panting furiously. This was not a pretty sight.

Finally, the nurse announced it was time to head into the delivery room. I felt numb and strange. Phil talked loudly to get my attention. At one point, the nurse started fidgeting as the monitor showed the heartbeat dropping quickly.

"Come on Bernadette—push with this contraction!" the doctor ordered. Phil grabbed my right arm and the nurse my left, and they added support as I pushed with all my strength.

"I can't do it," I cried. But another contraction was on me.

"Now, Bernadette, make this count. You *can* do it!" Dr. King said.

Frantically, I looked around between breaths. "Where's Phil?" He was still holding my hand, but he'd dropped to his knees, pleading for God's assistance and mercy.

And with that assurance, I squeezed his hand and pushed that baby out with all the strength I had left.

"I see a head! I see shoulders!" Dr. King shouted as he gently eased the child out.

There was no cry. He quickly suctioned the baby's mouth and began rubbing its back vigorously.

The silence was intense. Then he turned her over—her—our little girl. I heard the most wonderful sound. My little girl began to cry.

Our first daughter—and our sixth child, Alicia Marguerite Keaggy, was alive...and healthy.

When I finally got to hold my baby, it was as if a piece of heaven and earth were wrapped up snugly within my arms. Tears rolled down our cheeks into the cracks of our smiles.

Later, when I was settled back in my room, they brought Alicia in, all cleaned up and wrapped in pink. Phil laid her on the bed, and we lovingly examined every inch of her five-pound, nine-ounce little body—so beautiful and perfectly formed. We were in awe of God's creation before us.

I did not feel at all awkward or clumsy with her, but like a well-rehearsed athlete finally getting to play the real game. Phil, as well, handled this tiny one as if he'd been a papa for a very long time. She captured our hearts as I held her close and nursed her for the first time. How amazing that she instinctively knew what to do.

As is common in newborns, Alicia became jaundiced. My heart ached as I watched her under the lights with cotton patches taped over her eyes. Dr. King explained the necessity of this until her liver started functioning properly. By the fourth day, though, I was told it might be best to stop nursing for a few days and go home, leaving Alicia until her condition cleared up.

No way, I thought. I was determined not to leave that hospital without her. *Not this time.* Dr. King understood.

On the eighth day, Alicia's bilirubin count dropped to safe levels, and we packed up and headed home. We were a family...and we felt privileged to be one.

$\bigwedge$t home, Phil wrote a lullaby for Alicia called "Spend My Life With You." We lulled her to sleep many nights with this song:

> *Lay me down to rest,*
> *sing me a sweet lullaby—*
> *when will I see you again?*
> *Sleep come over me.*
>
> *Can't keep from closing my eyes*
> *The day is gone, but you'll carry on*
> *Watching, protecting me into the dawn*
> *Then another day to spend my life with you.*
>
> *'Cause there's a hope in my heart*
> *And I believe the day is coming*
> *When we'll never be apart*

Just to be where you are
And to spend my life with you
Would be a perfect start.

See you when I rise
Morning will bring me your song
Over and over again
Shine your light on me
Wash me in resplendent love
There is no shame with you as my aim
Yesterday, today, forever the same
And I only want to spend my life with you.
In your presence, Lord
There I will be satisfied
Over and over again.

As we went through our first weeks and months with Alicia, I realized how much had changed inside of us. We lived with a new resolve that God really was sovereign—with a wisdom far beyond ours. Even when things do not turn out exactly as we hope or plan we can rest in knowing that, somehow, it is part of his bigger plan.

I wanted to guard my heart now, and not let it close off again in a self-satisfied little world of motherhood. Maybe God's purpose in allowing all our losses was about to come clear. If so, I didn't want to miss it.

10

God works—if we allow him

Our experience of losing children remained with us long after Alicia was born. Going through painful times gives you compassion for those in pain. It causes you to take your eyes off yourself and reach out to others. At least I hoped this would be true for us.

When Phil put together a new band for an upcoming tour, we got to know Jerry, the drummer, and his wife, Grace, who was very pregnant at the time. Both were excited about their new addition to come.

When the delivery finally took place, however, Grace gave birth to a full-term, stillborn child. My heart ached for them, as Jerry told us the news over the phone. Cautiously, I called Grace, and shared in her pain and cried with her. Then I prayed for her too. I encouraged her to call me whenever she needed someone to talk to. Many evenings, Grace did call. I suggested she write down her feelings—the good *and* the bad ones—to help her sort through her emotions. I also encouraged her to seek out a group of people who met through the local hospital to share their similar experiences and to comfort one another. I knew this was important because, as Paul reminds us, we are to "carry each other's burdens, and in this way you will fulfill the law of Christ" (Galatians 6:2).

And the law of Christ is to love—even when it is difficult or uncomfortable.

How well I know these things. How much it cost to learn them.

It's easy to become caught up in our own lives that we don't look out for each other. The truth is, a five-minute phone call or a short note in the mail may be all that a desperate or lonely person needs that day to keep them from utter despair.

Why do we so quickly, easily, close off from others? Why do we forget that when someone is in the midst of difficulty and pain, survival becomes all consuming? During those times, we can hardly see through the dark cloud that surrounds us. We become incapable of dealing with our own needs. That's when we need true friends to be there for us, emotionally and in practical ways.

A small offer of love is all it takes to communicate, "You're special. You're important. You're worth taking the time for. You're not a failure."

There are inner lessons, of course, that we can only learn on our own.

Part of growing up is learning that death is going to be part of life. So often we simply refuse to deal with death, so we deny ourselves and others the time to grieve.

When Alicia was about five months old, our dear friend Bruce Coleman died—a slow, painful death—leaving behind his wife, Nancy, and two small children. Our own experiences with loss gave us a small glimpse of what it must be like to lose a wonderful husband of many years. We empathized with Nancy and tried to help her in tangible ways. During the months following Bruce's death, we talked often—any time, day or night, that she needed to. We shared dinners, and went for walks. Sometimes, when fear and loneliness became too much to bear, Nancy and the children spent the night with us in our home.

The healing process, we knew, is as slow and painful as death itself. After the initial trauma everyone else seems to move on with their lives—everyone but you. Too often we can try to quickly fill that loveless void with something else. But God works on our hearts in a much slower, unique pattern—if we allow him to.

Other truths we learned during those years of heartache proved invaluable. We had grown up—and learned strong lessons about life and faith in the midst of pain.

As I look at it now, I can see that God was acting like a father—on his knees at one end of the room, prodding his infant daughter to walk to him. *"You can do it, Bernadette. Come to Papa. I'll catch you! I'm here for you."* Sometimes we have to stretch our hands so far for help. And God may not pick us up on the first fall, but allow us to get up ourselves and press on.

Why? Because life is not a black-and-white matter, but full of gray areas. When there are many questions, and the answers are vague or nil, it causes us to stretch a little further to open ourselves to God until we understand that there are deeper shades of grace. As a mother, I soon realized that this little child was going to teach me new lessons about myself and life.

The focus was no longer on *me* or us as a couple; it was on raising a child in this world. We were now the responsible parties—and that in itself was pretty scary. In the past, God had used our painful experiences to draw us to him. Now it was this little child and the responsibility of being parents that brought us continually to our knees. Phil spent some sleepless nights struggling with his sense of insufficiency as a father to fully provide for the child God had given us.

For me, fear was still an occasional battle.

One night in particular, when Phil was due back late from a concert, I'd put Alicia to bed and settled down to read a book. A warm, still air crept through the open window—and then came the loud interruption of police loudspeakers in the streets. They urged everyone to go into their basements, because a tornado had been sighted two blocks from our home.

I jumped up, ran to Alicia's room and whisked her from her crib, then grabbed a radio on my way to the basement. We waited in the darkness for what seemed like an hour, hearing only rustling trees and heavy winds. Again and again, fear tried to grip me. I forced myself to focus on God, to rest myself *and* my child in him.

When the radio said the coast was clear, we crept upstairs. Everything seemed intact, but several blocks away, the tornado had left a path of devastation. I felt grateful for God's covering and mercy.

We now recognized the constant reminders of who really controls the universe and our destiny. Faith is not the belief that God will deliver what we want when we want it, but that he has gracious control of our lives and that he will be faithful to direct our paths and give us the grace to walk through life's unpredictable times. Lamentations 3:22-23 says: "God's compassions never fail. They are new every morning."

Mercy and grace enough for each day—that is what we are promised. And it is enough.

As time passed, Phil and I were quite happy to discover that I was pregnant again. Alicia was three years old at the time, and we felt she was ready to be dethroned, or at least to have a little companion at her side. But just because I had successfully given birth to Alicia, didn't mean this time would be the same.

I walked through it cautiously, taking it a day at a time. My inward battle between trust and fear intensified during the second trimester. To top it off, we were moving again—this time to California. It meant packing and traveling and added stress.

Dr. King searched out one of the best high-risk pregnancy specialists in Orange County, California, and once we'd moved I went to meet with him. Dr. Goldstein would be doing the surgery this time and monitoring this pregnancy. This time I required higher dosages of drugs and more bed rest, but we made it through.

In my eighth month—on February 14, 1984—Olivia Anne, a gift from God, was born. We felt it significant that Olivia was born fourteen years to the day after Phil's mom was in a car accident that took her life. Each year, Valentine's Day holds a double meaning for us— that life is taken away, but it is also given as a good gift from a Father who loves us.

After Olivia's birth, the doctor cautioned us about future pregnancies being more difficult. By God's grace, we were blessed with a second child, and we were more than content. We had no desire to push the limits to have a third.

So I was shocked when, in the fall of 1986, the nurse in my doctor's office called to tell me the results of the tests the doctor had ordered. "Mrs. Keaggy," she said, "the tests are positive. You are pregnant."

Admittedly, I was stunned. I hung up the phone without saying a word.

As I sat down heavily at the kitchen table, I faced that old tendency to want to seize control. *This is too scary,* I thought. *I don't want to go through all the emotional turmoil again. I can't deal with this.* It wasn't the thought of a third child that bothered me; it was the process of getting there that had become, each time, a more serious undertaking. Not to mention that I was now already chasing after two children.

Once again, there was no turning back. It was a long and slow pregnancy—and more difficult, as the doctor predicted.

I began having constant contractions in my sixth month. The doctor prescribed higher dosages of drugs, as well as some new ones. Even with the best of care, the outcome was uncertain again.

I was in and out of the hospital in my seventh month as the doctors tried to prolong this pregnancy. Finally, as I stabilized, I was sent home to rest in bed until the baby was due. Phil canceled weeks of concerts, and became Mr. Mom. My only outing was to the hospital for stress tests on the baby. There was no guarantee this baby would make it, and it was definitely taking an emotional toll on our family.

Now, though, Phil and I were battle-ready, and he was my constant support and help. He even learned to run the vacuum cleaner, and figured out the dishwasher. I must admit, our meals took an interesting turn as Chef Phil laced everything with garlic and cayenne pepper....

The last weeks brought us closer spiritually. And we gained new respect for the role each of us played in our marriage. Phil had a fresh appreciation for what it takes to run a busy household efficiently. For one thing, he had to deal with every mother's frustration of not staying on top of things, not being in control. And I had to let the messes be handled by someone else, while I lay flat in bed. That, for me, was harder than it sounds. Our little girls didn't understand why Mommy was in bed each day and couldn't be out running around with them. Papa was definitely doing overtime.

Over and over, I read Philippians 4:13: "I can do everything through him who gives me strength." This had come to mean to me that Christ is our strength when we are weak—physically, emotionally or spiritually.

Three weeks before his due date, Ian was born. Phil and I were thrilled to hold a healthy infant son in our arms at last.

One day we would tell him about his older brothers. But for now, he seemed content to be cradled in our arms.

Ian, Alicia and Olivia Keaggy

EPILOGUE

I know that our story isn't everyone's story. Not everyone who desires children will be blessed with them. I've found that experiencing the goodness of life has nothing to do with being "good enough," and everything to do with recognizing God's sovereignty. He is eternal, and will accomplish—in his way and time—what concerns us. It was only when Phil and I learned to dig deeply into ourselves and work through painful situations that we discovered what was really important. Pain, whether physical or emotional, takes its toll on our relationships and alienates us from others. If we're not careful it can close us off from God.

Scripture says, "Now we see but a poor reflection as in a mirror; then we shall see face to face" (1 Corinthians 13:12). When that day comes, I will have a multitude of questions to be answered—or maybe at that time they won't even matter. The veil will be lifted on all our disappointments of life.

Phil addressed this question in his song "All Our Wishes":

> *All our wishes can't be wrong,*
> *all our dreams between us two.*
> *There's a yearning in our song—*
> *wishing, believing that dreams come true.*

All our wishes can't be wrong,
all these dreams between us two.
There are others who know this song,
who know the meaning of its tune.

He kneels by her side,
places his hand where there was life.
This child this baby is gone.
She hears him say, "We'll carry on."

All our wishes can't be wrong,
all these dreams between us two.
We are not the only ones,
though it seems it's me and you.
Yet for now it's me and you...

Life is at times painful and sad, at other times it is full of peace and happiness. Doubt and anger can try to crush our trust in God, who offers unfailing love. "Come to me, all you who are weary and burdened, and I will give you rest" (Matthew 11:28), Jesus said. He has the strength to carry us through. When Phil and I cried out in pain and grief, Jesus listened. When we asked why, he understood. When we didn't have the strength to take the next step, he gently pushed us on.

You see, *answers* aren't the real issue. Clinging to God through all of life's circumstances and helping others to do the same—that is what's important. Knowing God is what made the difference for us.

Through it all, my hope is that I've become more open and vulnerable to God, and to others in their plight. Life's lessons never end—we can either gain wisdom and understanding from them or let them beat us down. I choose to learn and grow through life's circumstances—and it's a daily choice.

To quote from our friend C. S. Lewis:

> You never know how much you really believe anything until its truth or falsehood becomes a matter of life and death to you. It is easy to say you believe a rope to be strong and sound as long as you are merely using it to cord a box. But suppose you had to hang by that rope over a precipice. Wouldn't you then first discover how much you really trusted it? Only a real risk tests the reality of belief.

Based on what I know, I can tell you this: When you test the rope of God's grace, it will hold you. I promise.

RESOURCES

BOOKS

Sherokee Ilse and Linda H. Burns, *Empty Arms: A Guide to Help Parents and Loved Ones Cope with Miscarriage, Stillbirth and Neonatal Death* (Wintergreen, 1985)

C. S. Lewis, *A Grief Observed* (Faber and Faber, 1961)

Larry G. Peppers, Ph.D. and Ronald J. Knapp, Ph.D., *How to Go on Living After the Death of a Baby* (Peachtree Publishers, 1985)

Sheldon Vanauken, *A Severe Mercy* (Harper and Row, 1977)

Philip Yancey, *Disappointment with God* (Harper, 1988)

ORGANIZATIONS

AMEND (Aiding Mothers Experiencing Neonatal Death)
4324 Berrywick Terrace
St. Louis, MO 63128
314-487-7582

The Compassionate Friends
P.O. Box 3696
Oak Brook, IL 60521
312-990-0010

Empty Cradle (information and bimonthly newsletter)
4595 Mount King Drive
San Diego, CA 92117
619-692-2144

Grief Recovery Helpline
1-800-445-4808
(Monday through Friday, 9 a.m. to 5 p.m., Pacific Standard Time)

The Pregnancy and Infant Loss Center of Minnesota
1415 E. Wayzata Blvd., Suite 22
Wayzata, MN 55391
612-473-9372

Resolve
1310 Broadway
Somerville, MA 02144
617-623-1156

SHARE
St. Elizabeth's Hospital
211 S. Third St.
Belleville, IL 62222
618-234-2120

Sidelines (supporting women through difficult pregnancies)
c/o Candace Hurley
2805 Park Place
Laguna Beach, California 92651
714-593-6199

OTHER BOOKS FROM SPARROW PRESS

Michael Card
Come to the Cradle
The Promise

Keith Green
A Cry in the Wilderness

Melody Green and David Hazard
No Compromise: The Life Story of Keith Green

Steve Green
Hymns: A Portrait of Christ

Betsy Hernandez and Donny Monk
Silent Night: A Mouse Tale

Patrick Kavanaugh
A Taste for the Classics
The Spiritual Lives of Great Composers

Stormie Omartian
Better Body Management
Greater Health God's Way